Artificial Intelligence

OrangeBooks Publication

1st Floor, Rajhans Arcade, Mall Road, Kohka, Bhilai, Chhattisgarh 490020

Website: **www.orangebooks.in**

First Edition, 2026

ISBN: 978-93-7426-743-1

Price: Rs. 800.00

Printed in India

ARTIFICIAL INTELLIGENCE

DR. A.J.K. PRASAD
DR. GOWRAMMA G.S. | DR. REDDAPPA H.N.

OrangeBooks Publication
www.orangebooks.in

Preface – First Edition

It gives us immense pleasure to present the first edition of **"Artificial Intelligence"**, a textbook designed to provide a comprehensive yet accessible introduction to the fascinating and rapidly evolving field of Artificial Intelligence (AI). This book has been carefully structured with undergraduate students in mind, emphasizing clarity of concepts, logical progression of topics, and a balanced blend of theory and application.

Artificial Intelligence today plays a transformative role across diverse domains such as healthcare, transportation, communication, finance, manufacturing, and scientific research. Recognizing its growing importance, this textbook aims to equip learners with a strong conceptual foundation while nurturing analytical and problem-solving skills essential for advanced study and practical implementation.

The textbook is organized into **five chapters**, each thoughtfully developed to build a solid base and gradually introduce more advanced ideas. Special attention has been devoted to the inclusion of **relevant illustrations and well-structured tables**, which enhance comprehension and provide visual clarity to complex concepts. Every chapter concludes with **chapter summaries, conclusions,** encouraging students to reflect upon, analyze, and apply what they have learned. In addition, **and a set of carefully curated review questions, index** and **glossary** are provided at the end to facilitate quick reference and reinforce key terminology.

Chapter Breakdown

Chapter 1 – What is AI? Foundations and History of AI

This chapter lays the groundwork by exploring the origins, historical evolution, philosophical roots, and foundational principles of Artificial Intelligence. It establishes the context for understanding modern AI systems.

Includes 14 Figures and 2 Tables.

Chapter 2 – Agents and Environments: Intelligent Agents

A detailed exploration of intelligent agents, their environments, rationality, performance measures, and structural components. This chapter introduces the learner to the core building blocks of AI systems.

Includes 7 Figures and 2 Tables.

Chapter 3 – Uncertain Knowledge and Reasoning

This chapter addresses the challenges of decision-making under uncertainty. It introduces probability fundamentals, Bayes' Rule, independence, and inference techniques that enable intelligent reasoning in uncertain environments.

Includes 5 Figures and 1 Table.

Chapter 4 – Search and Search Strategies

A comprehensive discussion on problem-solving through search techniques, covering both uninformed and informed search strategies along with an introduction to logical agents.

Includes 2 Figures and 4 Tables.

Chapter 5 – Knowledge-Based Agents

The final chapter focuses on knowledge representation, propositional and first-order logic, inference mechanisms, and reasoning techniques that empower intelligent systems to make informed decisions.

Includes 7 Figures and 5 Tables.

The collective effort behind this textbook reflects our commitment to academic excellence and our sincere intention to foster a deeper understanding of Artificial Intelligence among undergraduate learners. We hope this book will serve not only as a classroom guide but also as a dependable reference for students and educators alike.

We welcome constructive feedback from readers, which will help us refine and enhance future editions to meet evolving academic and technological needs. It is worth mentioning that all Figures in this textbook have been redrawn using licensed software. We also gratefully acknowledge the use of two icons in Figure 4.1, which have been duly credited in the text.

Sincerely,
The Authors

Acknowledgements

Firstly, we express our gratitude to the Almighty for blessing us with the opportunity to write this book. We extend our heartfelt thanks to the management of Don Bosco Institute of Technology and the Rajya Vokkaligara Sangha, Bengaluru, for their unwavering support and encouragement.

We would like to sincerely thank **Dr. B.S. Nagabhushana**, Principal of Don Bosco Institute of Technology, and **Dr. J. Prakash**, Principal of Bangalore Institute of Technology, Bengaluru, for their guidance and motivation throughout this endeavour.

Dr. Gowramma G. S. expresses her sincere gratitude to her family members, **Mr. Basavaraj N. Nashipudi and Akshata Nashipudi,** for their support and understanding. But for which accomplishment of bringing this book to present shape is not possible

Dr. Reddappa H.N. expresses his deepest gratitude to his family members, **Mrs. Dharani S**. and **Diganth R**., for their unending support and encouragement.

Dr. A.J.K. Prasad is profoundly thankful to **Venkata Lakshmi**, **Aparna**, and **Jyotsna** for their continuous support, encouragement, and understanding throughout this endeavour.

We extend our indebted thanks to our colleagues for their invaluable encouragement and timely support. We also acknowledge Mr. Kushal for his assistance in creating some of the illustrations featured in this book.

We sincerely appreciate the developers and promoters of OpenAI, Sonnet Claude AI, Perplexity AI, Grok AI, DeepSeek AI, and iMathEQ.com for their invaluable tools that significantly aided in clarifying complex concepts, generating SVGs, and providing Python code for visuals and equations. Their contributions have been indispensable to the success of this project, and we extend our heartfelt thanks to all the team members behind these remarkable platforms.

We express our sincere gratitude to OrangeBooks Publishing (Orangebooks.in) for publishing this book in such an elegant format. Our special thanks go to Madhavi, Payal Ghosh, Preeti Shetty, and their team for their editorial support and dedication.

Dr. A.J.K. Prasad

Dr. Gowramma G. S.

Dr. Reddappa H.N.

Dedication

This book is dedicated to our teachers, whose guidance and wisdom have shaped us, and to our students, whose curiosity and enthusiasm inspire us to remain focused and committed to lifelong learning

Contents

List of Figures

List of Tables

Chapter – 1

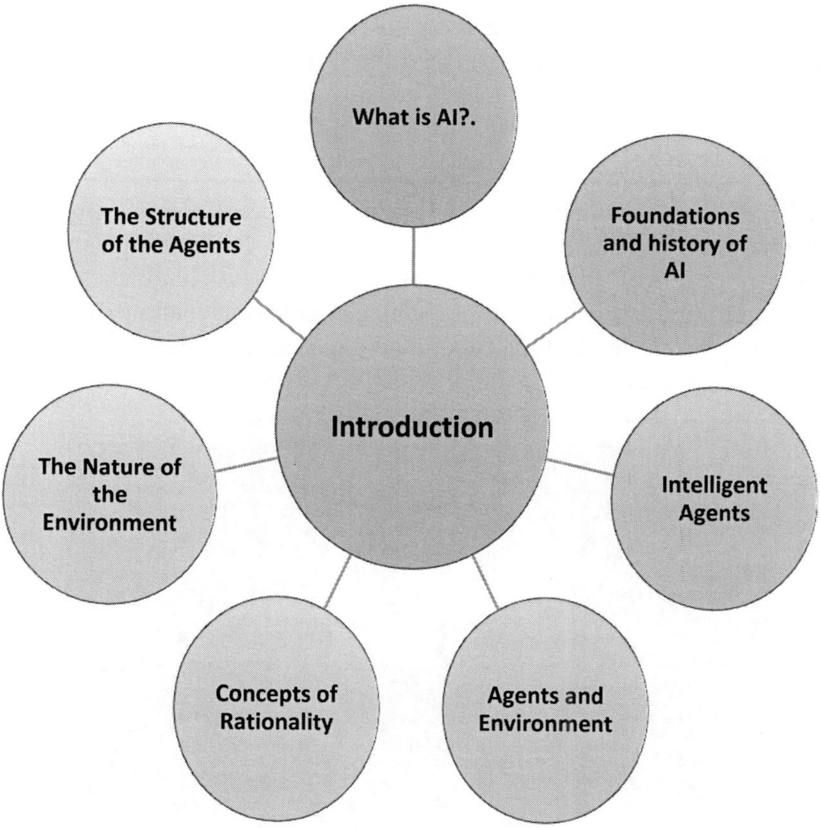
What is AI?.
Foundations and history of AI
Intelligent Agents
Agents and Environment
Concepts of Rationality
The Nature of the Environment
The Structure of the Agents
Introduction

Introduction

Artificial Intelligence (AI) refers to the simulation of human intelligence. in machines that are Artificial Intelligence (AI) refers to the simulation of human intelligence in machines that are programmed to think and act like humans. It involves the development of algorithms and computer programs that can perform tasks that typically require human intelligence, such as visual perception, speech recognition, decision-making, and language translation. AI has the potential to revolutionize many industries and has a wide range of applications, from virtual personal assistants to AI agents Multi-Agent. Systems to self-driving cars.

1.0 What is AI?

Artificially created Intelligence (AI) is the science of creating machines that think and act like humans or human beings, having foundations in computer science, mathematics, psychology, and linguistics. With significant studies in disciplines/subjects covering natural language processing, machine learning, robotics, and computer vision, AI will have evolved from early fundamental principles to innovative triumphs by 2024, changing industries and our daily life.

Figure 1.1 Artificial Intelligence

(Figure generated from the webpage https://deepai.org)

We, the human beings, call ourselves ***Homo sapiens*** — *man the wise* — because our **intelligence**. is so important to us. (*Homo sapiens*: the primate species to which modern humans belong; regarded as a species). For thousands of years we have tried to understand **how we think** — how a mere handful of matter can perceive, understand, predict, and manipulate a world **far larger and more complicated than itself- The Universe**. The field of **Artificial Intelligence (AI)** goes further still; it attempts not just to understand but also to **Build Intelligent Entities**.

AI currently encompasses a **huge variety of subfields**, ranging from general learning and perception, to the specific such as chess playing, proving mathematical theorems, writing, poetry, driving a car on a crowed street and diagnosing disease. AI is relevant to any field intellectual task; it is truly a universal field.

It is appropriate to understand the meaning of artificial intelligence. before delving into the subject of Artificial Intelligence. Let us first understand the meaning of intelligence:

1.1 The Four Kingdoms: Mineral, Plant, Animal, and Human Kingdoms

The intellectual capacity of the mineral kingdom is low, plants display considerable intelligence. through their capacity to grow and reproduce. Animals show more advancement through qualities that include growth, reproduction, and mobility. Among all of these kingdoms, humans surpass the others in intelligence, creativity, invention, and being able to use the other three for benefiting society.

1.1.2 Intelligence: Intelligence has been defined in a number of ways, encompassing being able to abstract, logic, understand self-awareness, learn, understand feelings reason, plan, be creative, think critically, and handle problems. It can be described as the ability to gain or infer information and retain it as knowledge that can be applied to adaptive behaviours within an environment. or environment.

1.2 Definitions of AI

8 definitions of AI are given in the following list and are laid out along two dimensions —

1. **Humanly**
2. **Rationally**

Some definitions of AI organized into 4 categories:

- Thinking Humanly
- Thinking Rationally
- Acting Humanly
- Acting Rationally

In table 1.1 Four Perspectives of Artificial Intelligence are presented (source Russell and Norvig)

Table 1.1 Four Perspectives of Artificial Intelligence

Thinking Humanly	Thinking Rationally
Concerned with thought processes & reasoning	
1. The exciting new effort to make computers think… machines with minds, in the full and literal sense." **Haugeland, 1985.**	**2.** The study of mental faculties through the use of computational models." **Charniak and McDermott, 1985.**
3. The automation of activities that we associate with human thinking, activities such as decision-making, problem-solving, learning. **Bellman, 1978**.	**4.** The study of computations that make it possible to perceive, reason and act. **"Winston, 1992.**
Acting Humanly	**Acting Rationally**
5. The art of creating machines that performs functions that require intelligence. when performed by people." **Kurzweil, 1990**	**6.** Computational intelligence. is the study or design of intelligent agents." **Poole et al., 1998**
7. The study of how to make computers do things at which people are better. **"Rich and Knight, 1991**	**8.** AI is concerned with intelligent behaviour in artefacts **Nilsson, 1998**

1.2.1 Definitions Based on Behaviour

<table>
<tr><td rowspan="2">Left Measure success in terms of fidelity to human performance.</td><td colspan="2">To Thought process & reasoning</td><td rowspan="2">Right Measure against an ideal performance measure.</td></tr>
<tr><td>Bottom Behaviour</td><td>Bottom</td></tr>
</table>

Historically, all four approaches to AI have been followed, each by different people with different methods. A human-cantered approach must be in part an empirical science, involving observing observations and hypotheses about human behaviour. A rationalist's approach involves a combination of mathematics and engineering. The various groups have been disparaged (regarded or represent as being of title worth- be title denigrate etc.) and helped each other → then.

Let's Now Explore the Definitions as Envisioned by Different Scents

1. **Explanations. Thinking Humanly:** The ability of machines to think like humans, mimicking human cognitive processes. "The exciting new effort to make computers think.. machines with minds, in the full and literal sense." (Haugeland, 1985) & "[The automation of] activities that we associate with human thinking, activities such as decision-making, problem solving, learning.." (Bellman, 1978)

2. **Thinking Rationally**: The logical reasoning approach where machines aim to think according to ideal rationality. "The study of mental faculties through the use of computational models." (Charniak and McDermott, 1985) & The study of the computations that make it possible to perceive, reason, and act." (Winston, 1992)

3. **Acting Humanly** Machines perform actions that imitate human behaviour (e.g., passing the Turing Test). "The art of creating machines that performs functions that require intelligence. when performed by people." (Kurzweil, 1990) & "The study of how to

make computers do things at which, at the moment, people are better.” (Rich and Knight, 1991) &

4. **Acting Rationally**: Machines act to achieve the best outcome or an optimal performance measure based on rationality. “Computational Intelligence is the study of the design of intelligent agents.” (Poole et al., 1998) & the intelligent behaviour in artifacts.” (Nilsson, 1998)

Today, modern dictionary definitions highlight AI as a subfield of computer science and how machines might mimic human intellect (being human-like rather than being human).

Intelligence and continues to inspire new research and developments in this area.

1.2.2 “Thinking Humanly” – The Cognitive Modelling Approach

The interdisciplinary field of **Cognitive Science** brings together computer models from AI and experimental techniques from **Psychology** to construct precise and testable theories of the human mind. Cognitive science is a fascinating field, worthy of several textbooks in itself (Encyclopedia, Wilson & Keil, 1999). Real cognitive science is, however, based on **experimental investigations** of actual human or animals. etc, becomes possible.

Once we have sufficiently precise theories of human thinking →They must be expressed as **computer programs (CP)**.

- Given a computer program (CP) that thinks like a human,
- And given human data → we must have some ways of determining **How humans think?**

We need to get inside the actual **working of the human minds**.

There are three ways to find how the human mind works:

1. **Try to catch our own thoughts as they go by**
2. **Through psychological experiments**
3. **Through brain imaging/observation**

1.2.3. Thinking Rationally: The Laws of Thought Approach

The Greek philosopher Aristotle was the first to codify **"RIGHT THINKING"** is irrefutable reasoning process. Aristotle's **"Syllogisms"– deductive reasoning→** always yielded correct conclusions when given correct premises. **For example, Socrates is a man. All men are mortal. Therefore, Socrates is mortal.**

These laws of thought were supposed to govern the operations of mind; their study initiated the field of **Logic.**) **Logicians (19th century).** Figure 1.2 illustrates the progression from Aristotle's syllogistic reasoning to 19th-century formal logic notation and ultimately to 1965's general-purpose problem-solving programs, demonstrating how the formalization of logical thought evolved from philosophical principles to computational systems capable of addressing any solvable problem.

The Development of formal Reasoning System

- A precise symbolic notation was developed to represent statements about all kinds of objects that could, in principle, exist in the world and the relationships among them.
- Arithmetic notation, in contrast, provides statements only about **numbers**.
- Programs were created with the aim of solving any problem that is, in theory, solvable.

Figure 1.2 Evolution from Aristotelian logic to Computational Problem-Solving: The Development of Formal Reasoning Systems.

The so-called (**Logicist**. tradition within artificial intelligence. hopes to build/create an **Intelligent System**.

The Two Obstacles in Creating an Intelligent System:

Stating informal knowledge in formal terms problem required by **Logic Notation,** especially when the knowledge is less than **100% certain.**

the big difference between solving a **"in principle"** and **"solving in practice."**

A few 100 facts can exhaust the computational resources of any computer unless it has guidance as to which reasoning steps to try first.

Figure1.3 Key Challenges Facing the Logicist. Approach to Artificial Intelligence.

While the logicist approach to AI seeks to build intelligent systems through formal logic, Figure 13 highlights its two primary challenges: the difficulty of expressing informal, uncertain knowledge in formal logical terms, and the substantial gap between theoretical solvability and practical computational feasibility.

1.2.4 "Acting Humanly" The Turing Test

The Turing test, proposed by Alan Turing (1950), was designed to provide a satisfactory operational definition of **Intelligence**. A computer passes the test if a human interrogator, after asking some written questions, cannot tell whether the written responses come from a person or a computer.

Detailed understanding of the Turing test, we can note that **programming a computer to pass a rigorously applied test** provides plenty to work on.

The Computer Would Need To Possess The Following Capabilities:

1) **Natural Language Processing:**

   To enable it to communicate successfully in **English / any other natural language.**

2) **Knowledge Representation:**

   To store what it knows or hears.

3) **Automated Reasoning:**

   To use the stored information to answer questions and to draw new conclusions.

4) **Machine Learning:**

   To adapt to new circumstances and to detect and extrapolate patterns.

Turing test deliberately avoided direct physical interaction between the interrogator and the computer, because physical simulation of a person is unnecessary for intelligence.

However, the so-called **Total Turing Test** includes a video signal, so that the interrogator can test the subject's perceptual abilities, as well as the ability of the interrogator to pass physical objects **"through the hatch."**

To pass the Total Turing Test, a computer system must demonstrate intelligence. indistinguishable from a human across all modalities of interaction, not merely through text-based conversation. As illustrated in Figure 1.4, this requires the integration of computer vision capabilities to perceive and interpret objects in the environment., along with robotics systems that enable physical manipulation of those objects and autonomous navigation through space. These components extend the original Turing Test's scope from purely linguistic competence to embodied intelligence that can interact with the physical world in ways comparable to human capabilities.

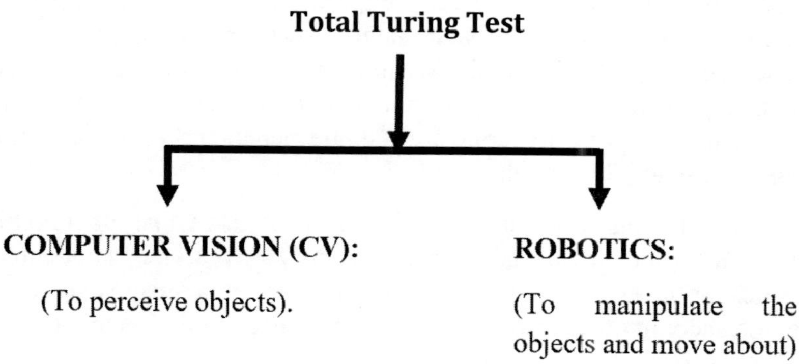

Figure 1.4 Components Required for a Computer to Pass the Total Turing Test"

"Driverless cars" would be a part of the Total Turing Test insofar as perceiving objects and manoeuvring in any road conditions, any terrain, and any season—rainy, foggy, snowy, to name a few.

1.2.5 The Six Disciplines

1. Natural Language Processing (NLP)

→ To process language.

2. Knowledge Representation

→ First Order Logic (FOL), Propositional logic.

3. Automated Reasoning

→ To process available information to reason/draw new conclusions.

4. Machine Learning (ML)

→ To detect and extrapolate patterns.

5. Computer Vision

→ To perceive objects.

6. Robotics.

→ To manipulate objects and move about.

These six disciplines comprise most of **Artificial Intelligence (AI)**, and the **Turing Test** deserves credit for proposing an evaluation method that remains relevant even 60–70 years later. However, AI researchers have not focused primarily on merely passing the (Total) Turing Test. Instead, they have prioritized studying the fundamental principles of intelligence rather than attempting to replicate a single benchmark—**the exemplar being the Turing Test itself**.

While the Turing Test has been used as **a measure of machine intelligence**. for over 6 decades (more precisely 74 years), it is not without its critics. Some argue that the test is too focused on language and doesn't take into account other **important aspects of intelligence.**, such as:

- **a)** Perception
- **b)** Problem-solving

c) Decision-making

Despite its limitations, the **Turing Test** remains an important reference point in the field of Artificial

1.2.6 Acting Rationally: The Rational Agent Approach

The concept of an agent—**derived from the Latin "one who acts"**—forms a cornerstone of modern AI system design. While all computer programs execution actions, Figure 1.5 distinguishes intelligent agents by their enhanced capabilities that extend far beyond simple task execution. An intelligent agent must operate autonomously without constant human intervention, perceive and interpret its environment. through sensors (as an example for Mars rover agents), persist over extended time periods while making logical decisions, adapt dynamically to changing conditions, and proactively create and pursue goals. This agent-based approach represents a paradigm shift from traditional programming, where the focus moves from explicitly coded responses to systems capable of flexible, goal-directed behaviour in complex, uncertain environments.

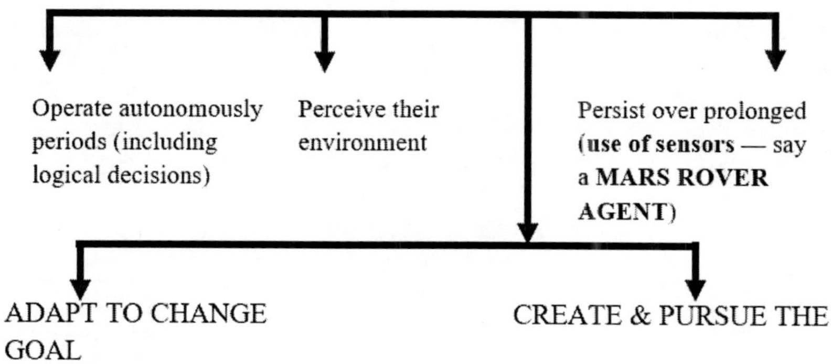

Figure 1.5 Defining Characteristics of an Intelligent Agent in Artificial Intelligence

1.3 The Foundations of AI and History of AI

Artificial intelligence. is fundamentally interdisciplinary, drawing upon diverse fields that converge to create systems capable of mimicking human intelligence. As illustrated in Figure 1.6, AI's theoretical and methodological foundations emerge from the synthesis of multiple disciplines: computer science and engineering provide the algorithmic infrastructure and computational frameworks; mathematics and statistics offer tools for logic, optimization, and probabilistic reasoning; neuroscience and biology inform our understanding of cognitive processes and neural architectures; psychology contributes models of human behaviour and learning; philosophy addresses questions of reasoning, consciousness, and ethical implications; economics supplies decision-making frameworks and utility. theory; linguistics enables natural language understanding; and cybernetics and control theory provide principles for feedback systems and autonomous behaviour. This rich interdisciplinary convergence ensures that AI systems are not only technically robust but also adaptable, ethically grounded, and aligned with diverse human needs and contexts.

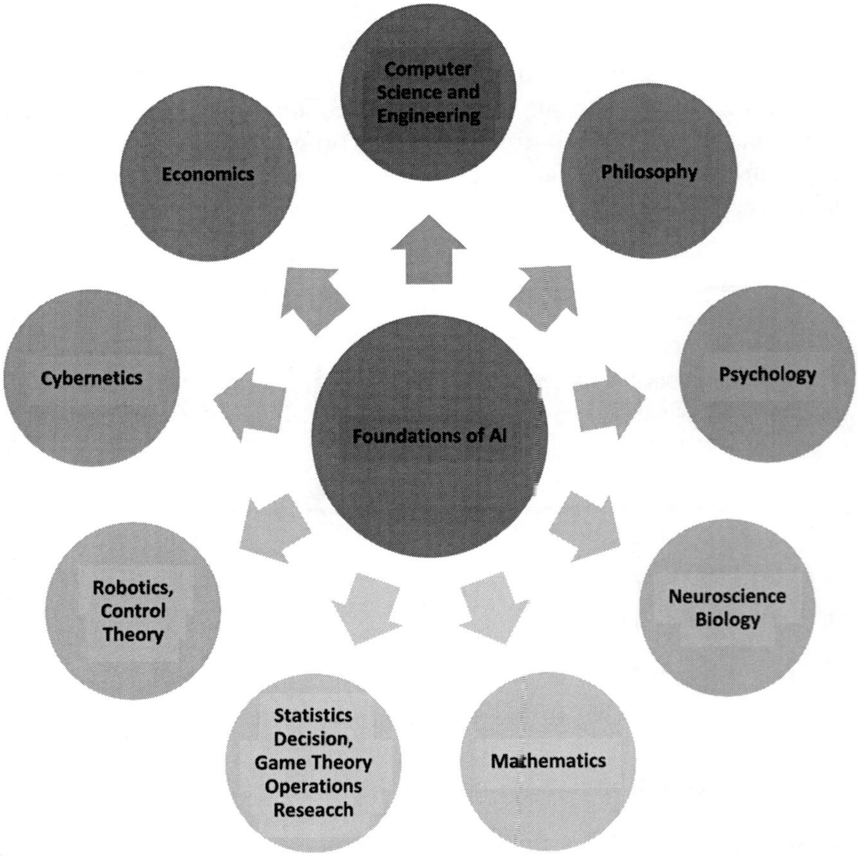

Figure 1.6 Foundations of Artificial Intelligence

Artificial intelligence. benefits from the distinct and crucial viewpoints that each contributing discipline offers. Philosophy, from Aristotle's formal logic to current discussions on machine consciousness and moral agency, offers the epistemological framework for comprehending knowledge representation, reasoning, and the central question of what intelligence itself is. The quantitative foundation of AI is found in mathematics and statistics, which provide the tools for probability theory, calculus, linear algebra, and optimization algorithms that drive machine learning models. Artificial neural networks, reinforcement learning paradigms, and cognitive architectures that aim to mimic human perception, memory, and decision-making processes are all influenced by neuroscience and psychology, which provide insights into how biological intelligence functions. Linguistics, meanwhile, provides the syntax, semantics, and pragmatics theories necessary for natural language processing, allowing machines to understand and generate human language with increasing sophistication.

The practical infrastructure for deploying AI is provided by engineering and systems-oriented disciplines. From search algorithms to deep learning frameworks, computer science and engineering provide the algorithms, data structures, programming paradigms, and computational architectures required to create functional AI systems. Game theory, utility. theory, and decision-making models under uncertainty—all essential to multi-agent systems and rational agent design—come from economics. Robots and autonomous cars can safely interact with dynamic situations thanks to the principles of feedback, stability, and autonomous system behaviour provided by control theory and cybernetics. This interdisciplinary synthesis is not just additive but also synergistic: developments in one field frequently spur innovations in others, resulting in a rich ecosystem of concepts that consistently pushes the limits of what artificial intelligence. is capable of. Anyone who wants to understand the possibilities and limitations of contemporary AI systems must have a solid understanding of these foundational contributions.

1.3.1 History of AI

1.3.1.1 The Genesis: Early Foundations (1940s-1950s)

The seeds of artificial intelligence. were planted in the mid-20th century when visionary thinkers began to imagine machines that could think. In 1950, British mathematician Alan Turing published a groundbreaking paper that introduced the concept of a "thinking machine" and proposed what would become known as the Turing Test—a method to evaluate whether a machine could exhibit intelligent behaviour indistinguishable from a human. This period laid the computational foundations that would support all future AI research. The excitement culminated in the summer of 1956 at the Dartmouth Conference, a historic gathering where computer scientist John McCarthy formally coined the term 'Artificial Intelligence." This conference marked the official birth of AI as a distinct field of scientific inquiry, bringing together researchers who believed that human intelligence could be precisely described and potentially replicated by machines.

1.3.2 The Turing Era

A major intellectual milestone in AI history was Alan Turing's seminal 1950 paper, *"Computing Machinery and Intelligence."* In this work, Turing posed the famous question, *"Can machines think?"* and proposed what later became known as the **Turing Test**. The test evaluates a machine's intelligence. based on its ability to exhibit human-like conversational behaviour. Turing's ideas established the philosophical and computational foundations of AI, framing intelligence as something that could be observed through behaviour rather than internal mechanisms.

1.3.3 Birth of Artificial Intelligence as a Field (1956)

Artificial Intelligence emerged as a formal research discipline in 1956 at the **Dartmouth Summer Research Conference on Artificial Intelligence**. During this landmark event, John McCarthy coined the term *"Artificial Intelligence."* Researchers at the conference expressed optimism that human-level intelligence. could be achieved within a few decades. This period marked the beginning of AI as an organized scientific field with dedicated goals, funding, and academic interest.

1.3.4 The Pioneering Years: Symbolic AI (1950s–1970s)

Between the 1950s and 1970s, AI research focused primarily on **symbolic reasoning**, also known as *Good Old-Fashioned AI (GOFAI)*. Early systems attempted to represent human knowledge using symbols and logical rules. Notable achievements included the **Logic Theorist**, which proved mathematical theorems, and the **General Problem Solver (GPS)**, designed to solve a wide range of problems using logical reasoning. While these systems demonstrated promise, they struggled with real-world complexity and uncertainty.

1.3.5 The AI Winter Period (1970s–1980s)

Despite early optimism, AI research encountered significant challenges during the 1970s and 1980s, leading to periods known as **AI winters**. Funding agencies reduced support due to unmet expectations, limited computational resources, and poor scalability of symbolic systems. These setbacks slowed research momentum and highlighted the gap between theoretical models and practical intelligence.

1.3.6 The Expert Systems Era (1980s)

The 1980s witnessed a resurgence of AI through **expert systems**, which captured human expertise in the form of rule-based decision systems. Prominent examples include **MYCIN**, used for medical diagnosis, and **DENDRAL**, applied in chemical analysis. These systems found success in industrial and commercial applications, demonstrating that AI could deliver tangible value when applied to well-defined domains.

1.3.7 Evolution of Machine Learning (1990s–2000s)

During the 1990s and early 2000s, AI underwent a paradigm shift from rule-based reasoning to **machine learning**, where systems learned patterns directly from data. Advances in statistics, probability theory, and optimization methods enabled data-driven models to outperform symbolic approaches in many tasks. Increased computing power and the availability of large datasets further accelerated this transition.

1.3.8 The Modern AI Revolution (2010s–Present)

The modern era of AI has been shaped by breakthroughs in **deep learning** and neural networks. Innovations such as **Convolutional Neural Networks (CNNs)** revolutionized image processing, while the introduction of the **Transformer architecture** Err**or in 2017** transformed natural language processing. Models like BERT and later large language models demonstrated unprecedented performance across diverse AI tasks. Today, AI systems are deeply integrated into everyday technologies such as smartphones, search engines, and recommendation systems.

1.3.9 Key Milestones in AI Development

Several landmark achievements illustrate AI's rapid progress. IBM's **Deep Blue** defeated a world chess champion in 1997, **Watson** won the quiz show *Jeopardy!* in 2011, and **AlphaGo** defeated a human Go champion in 2016. The 2020s marked the rise of **Generative AI**, with models capable of producing human-like text, images, audio, and video.

1.3.10 Large Language Models and Multimodal AI

The emergence of **Large Language Models (LLMs)**, such as the GPT series, marked a new phase in AI development. These models demonstrated advanced reasoning, language understanding, and generative capabilities. Parallel advancements in **multimodal AI** enabled systems to process and generate combinations of text, images, speech, and video, as seen in models like DALL·E, Stable Diffusion, and modern multimodal assistants.

1.3.11 Agentic AI and Multi-Agent Systems

A recent and significant development in AI is the rise of **agentic AI**, where systems operate autonomously with goal-oriented behaviour. Multi-agent architectures enable collaboration among specialized agents, leading to collective problem-solving and emergent behaviours. Frameworks such as Microsoft AutoGen, Anthropic's Constitutional AI, and Google Deep Mind's GOAT framework represent active research directions in building responsible and scalable agent-based AI systems.

1.3.12 Contemporary Applications of Artificial Intelligence

AI today plays a transformative role across sectors including healthcare, finance, transportation, education, entertainment, scientific research, business intelligence, and creative industries. Applications range from medical diagnosis and drug discovery to autonomous vehicles, intelligent tutoring systems, predictive analytics, and content generation.

1.3.13 Challenges, Ethics, and Future Directions

Despite rapid progress, AI faces technical challenges such as scalability, coordination in multi-agent systems, and performance optimization. Ethical concerns—including transparency, accountability, and safety—are equally important. Future AI systems are expected to exhibit enhanced reasoning, dynamic adaptation, and improved human–agent collaboration, enabling integration into smart cities, healthcare systems, financial markets, and educational platforms.

Note to Learners

Artificial Intelligence is a rapidly evolving discipline. To stay current, students are encouraged to consult recent publications from trusted sources such as the **National Science Foundation (NSF)**, leading academic institutions, and industry research labs. Continuous learning is essential for understanding the technological, ethical, and societal implications of AI.

1.4 Intelligent Agents

The core components of artificial intelligence. are, ***intelligent agents*** which use sensors to observe their surroundings and actuators to respond to them in order to accomplish predetermined objectives. Based on its perceptions and innate knowledge, an agent is deemed intelligent if it chooses behaviours that optimize its performance measure. Intelligence in agents refers to logical behaviour—selecting the best course of action in a given circumstance—rather than necessarily implying human-like reasoning. Physical agents like robots and self-driving cars are examples of intelligent agents, as are software agents like recommendation engines and search engines.

An autonomous intelligent agent is able to modify its actions in response to experience and shifting external circumstances. Agents can be learned, utility.-based, goal-based, model-based, or simple reflex agents, depending on their level of intelligence. Over time, learning agents gain new information through interactions with their surroundings, which enhances their performance. The foundation for sophisticated applications like multi-agent systems, autonomous systems, and agentic AI is the increasing adoption of intelligent agents with decision-making, planning, and cooperative skills in modern AI systems.

1.4.1 Agents & Environment

An **agent** is an entity that perceives its environment. through sensors and acts upon that environment through actuators. A **rational agent** is one that does the *right thing*, meaning it selects actions that maximize the expected value of its performance measure, given the available percepts and knowledge. Rationality. depends on the agent's perception history, the actions it can perform, its built-in knowledge, and the goals it is designed to achieve. Rational behaviour does not imply perfection but reflects the best possible decision under given circumstances. A rational agent is one that does the *right thing.* An agent is anything that can be viewed as perceiving its environment through sensors and acting upon that environment through actuators. This concept of an agent in te context of artificial intelligence. is illustrated in Figure 1.7.

Agent = Agent Architecture + Agent Program

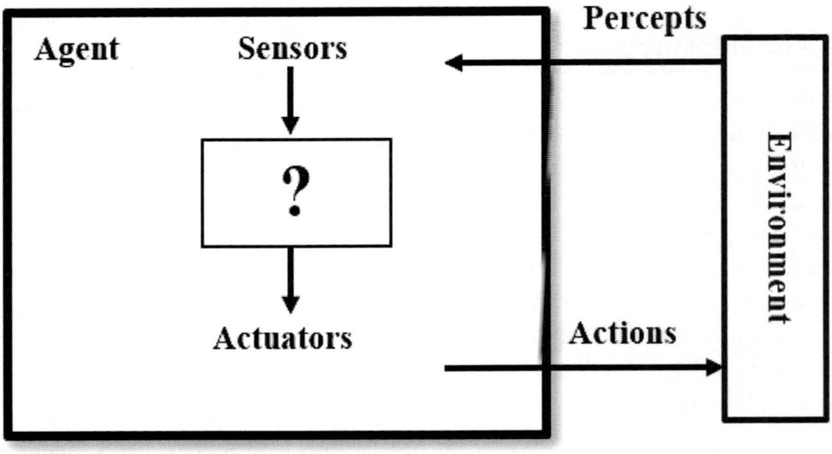

Figure 1.7 Agents Interact with Environments Through Sensors and Actuators.

1.4.2 Concept of Rationality.

Rationality. in Artificial Intelligence refers to the ability of an agent to select actions that maximize the expected performance measure, given the available perceptual information and knowledge about the environment. A rational agent does not necessarily possess complete knowledge or make perfect decisions; rather, it acts optimally based on what it has perceived so far and the actions it can perform. Rationality depends on the agent's performance measure, prior knowledge, percept sequence, and the set of possible actions. Thus, rational behaviour is defined not by always achieving success, but by consistently choosing actions that are expected to lead to the best possible outcome under uncertainty.

In Artificial Intelligence, *rationality.* refers to the ability of an agent to choose actions that lead to the best expected outcome, given the information available to it. According to its percept sequence, past knowledge, and the variety of possible actions/alternatives, a rational agent maximizes its performance measure. Rationality. emphasises making the best choices feasible in an environment. of uncertainty and limited resources rather than implying perfection or omniscience. Therefore, Thus, an agent may be rational even if its actions occasionally lead to failure, provided those actions were reasonable given the circumstances. The performance metric/measure that determines success, the agent's percept history, the actions it can take, and its environmental knowledge/details/data are the four main determinants of an agent's rationality. An agent can perform more logically if it has richer action capabilities, more accurate sensors, and better environmental models. Importantly, rationality is assessed in relation to the environment and design goals of the agent rather than by contrasting it with human intellect. Figure 1.8 depicts the four things which decide an agent's rational behaviour at any given time.

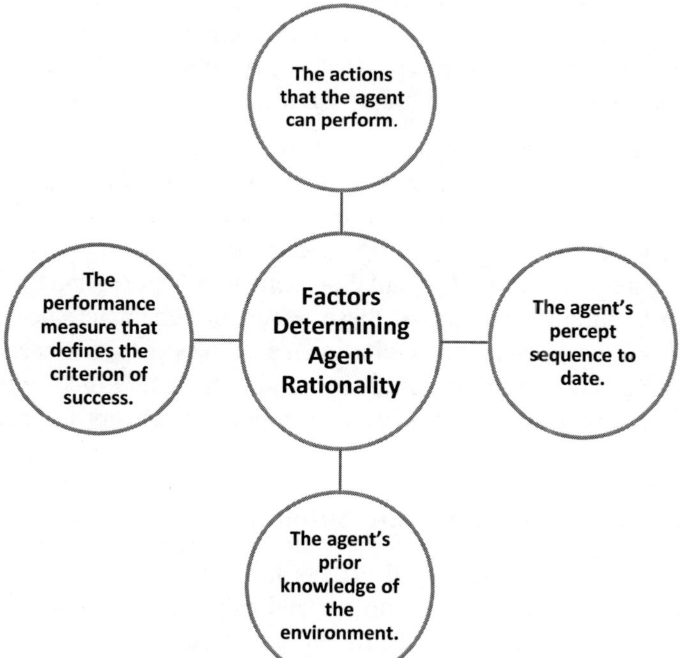

Figure 1.8 The Four Things That Determine Rationality/Rational Behaviour of An Agent I (The Concept Adapted from Russell Norvig).

It is important to distinguish rationality. from intelligence. Rationality. emphasizes consistent goal-directed behaviour, while intelligence encompasses learning, thinking, and ability to solve problems. Though a highly complex system might behave irrationally if it is unable to maximize its results, a simple reflex agent may be rational if it consistently meets its goals of performance in a clearly defined environment. Therefore, rationality serves as a foundational principle in AI, guiding the design and evaluation of intelligent agents across diverse applications.

1.5 The Nature of the Environment

The environment in artificial intelligence. refers to everything external to an intelligent agent with which it interacts while performing tasks. It provides the context in which an agent perceives information through sensors and acts using actuators. The nature of the environment determines how an agent perceives, reasons, and acts, and strongly influences the design of the agent, its behaviour, and its ability to achieve goals effectively. Environments may vary in terms of observability, determinism, episodic or sequential structure, dynamics, discreteness, and whether they involve single or multiple agents.

Intelligent agents confront different challenges in diverse environments. While some environments are simple and fully observable, others are dynamic, complex, uncertain, or hostile/adversarial, necessitating the use of memory, learning, planning, or agent coordination while performing tasks. AI researchers might select suitable agent architectures and methods for decision-making by looking at these contextual characteristics. This methodical categorization of environments serves as the basis for comprehending the different kinds of environments, which will be discussed in the part that follows. It is an important concept in artificial intelligence.

1.5.1 Omniscience, Learning, and Autonomy

In Artificial Intelligence, **rationality does not imply omniscience**. An omniscient agent would have complete and perfect knowledge of the environment and the outcomes of all possible actions. However, real-world environments are often uncertain, partially observable, and dynamic, making omniscience practically impossible. A rational AI agent is therefore not expected to know everything; instead, it is expected to act **optimally based on the information available to it at a given time**. Rationality. is judged by whether the agent chooses the best possible action given its percepts, knowledge, and limitations, not by whether it always produces the perfect outcome.

Learning plays a crucial role in enhancing rationality. over time. Since agents typically begin with incomplete knowledge, learning mechanisms allow them to improve their performance through experience. By observing the consequences of their actions and receiving feedback from the environment, learning agents update their internal models, decision rules, or utility estimates. This ability to learn enables agents to adapt to changing environments, handle uncertainty more effectively, and approach rational behaviour progressively, even when initial knowledge is limited. Thus, learning compensates for the lack of omniscience and is a key factor in sustaining long-term rationality.

Autonomy. refers to the extent to which an agent's behaviour is determined by its own experience rather than by pre-programmed instructions. A highly autonomous agent relies less on human intervention and more on its own percepts and learning capabilities to make decisions. Autonomy strengthens rationality by allowing agents to operate independently in complex and unpredictable environments. An autonomous agent that can learn from experience and act without constant external control is better equipped to behave rationally across diverse situations. Together, the absence of omniscience, the presence of learning, and a high degree of autonomy define practical rationality in intelligent agents.

1.5.2 Transition to Task Environment and Performance Measure, Environment, Actuators., Sensors Framework (PEAS.)

Agents form the core of Artificial Intelligence, representing systems that perceive their environment through sensors, reason about the available information, and act through actuators to achieve specific goals. As discussed earlier in this section, agents range from simple reflex agents to advanced learning and multi-agent systems, differing in their levels of autonomy, adaptability, and intelligence. Their behaviour is strongly influenced by the nature of the environment in which they operate—whether it is static or dynamic, deterministic or stochastic, fully observable or partially observable.

While the classification of environments helps us understand the general characteristics under which agents function, designing an intelligent agent for a real-world application requires a more precise and structured specification of the problem it must solve. This need leads to the concept of a **task environment**, which explicitly defines what the agent is expected to do, how it perceives its surroundings, what actions it can perform, and how its success is evaluated.

To systematically analyze and design intelligent agents within a task environment, Artificial Intelligence adopts the **PEAS framework**. PEAS provides a clear and organized method for describing an agent's operational context by identifying the criteria for success, the environment in which the agent operates, the actions it can take, and the information it can sense. Thus, the PEAS framework acts as a bridge between abstract environment classifications and practical agent implementation.

The **PEAS framework** is a standard tool in Artificial Intelligence used to formally specify an agent's task environment.. It helps designers clearly define the essential components required for building and evaluating intelligent agents.

The **Performance Measure** specifies the criteria used to evaluate how successfully an agent achieves its objectives. These measures depend on the application and may include accuracy, efficiency, safety, speed, or user satisfaction. The **Environment** represents the external world in which the agent operates and may be physical or virtual, simple or complex, static or dynamic. The **Actuators**. are the mechanisms through which the agent acts upon the environment., such as motors, displays, or control signals. The **Sensors**. allow the agent to perceive the environment by collecting relevant information, such as visual input, sound, temperature, or data streams.

By clearly defining these four components, the PEAS framework enables systematic comparison, analysis, and design of intelligent agents across diverse applications. It ensures that the agent's goals, capabilities, and operating conditions are explicitly stated, thereby facilitating effective and rational agent behaviour. In table 1.2 is presented a summary with examples of environments in ai and the corresponding PEAS (Performance, Environment, Actuators, and Sensors.) for agents.

Table 1.2 Summary with Examples of Environments in AI and the Corresponding PEAS (Performance, Environment, Actuators., and Sensors.) for agents

Example Environment	Performance Measure	Environment	Actuators	Sensors
Autonomous Vehicle	Safety, efficiency, speed, passenger comfort	Dynamic, partially observable, stochastic	Steering, throttle, brake, signal lights	Cameras, LIDAR, GPS, speedometer
Chess Playing Agent.	Win the game, minimize opponent score	Fully observable, deterministic, discrete	Move pieces on the board	Visual representation of the board
Vacuum Cleaner Agent.	Cleanliness of the room, minimal energy usage	Static/dynamic (depending on obstacles), partially observable, deterministic	Motors controlling suction and wheels	Dirt sensors., bump sensors, location sensors
Personal Assistant Agent.	Correctness and relevance of responses, user satisfaction	Partially observable, stochastic	Voice responses, text messages	Speech recognition, text input
Robotic Surgery System	Precision, safety, completion of surgical tasks	Static, fully observable, deterministic	Surgical instruments	Cameras, pressure sensors.
Stock Trading Agent.	Maximize portfolio return, minimize risk	Dynamic, partially observable, stochastic	Buy/sell orders	Market data feeds, historical prices
Search and Rescue Robot	Time efficiency, successful rescue	Dynamic, partially observable, stochastic	Robotic arms, wheels or treads, communication systems	Cameras, infrared sensors., environmental hazard detectors

Smart Thermostat	Maintain desired temperature with minimal energy consumption	Static, fully observable, deterministic	Heating or cooling controls	Temperature sensors., humidity sensors
Traffic Management System	Reduce congestion, optimize traffic flow	Dynamic, partially observable, stochastic	Traffic signals, variable message signs	Traffic cameras, vehicle sensors.
E-Commerce Recommendation System	Accuracy and relevance of recommendations, user engagement, conversion rates	Partially observable, stochastic	Display product suggestions	User behaviour data, purchase history, browsing patterns

1.5.3 Types of Environments

In Artificial Intelligence, an **environment**. refers to the external problem space within which an intelligent agent operates and to which it provides solutions. The characteristics of the environment significantly influence how an agent is designed, how it behaves, and how its performance is evaluated. Based on different properties and interaction patterns, AI environments can be classified into the following **ten major types**:

1. Fully Observable vs. Partially Observable
2. Deterministic vs. Stochastic
3. Competitive vs. Collaborative
4. Single-Agent vs. Multi-Agent
5. Static vs. Dynamic
6. Discrete vs. Continuous
7. Episodic vs. Sequential
8. Known vs. Unknown
9. Accessible vs. Inaccessible
10. Benign vs. Adversarial

Each classification highlights a specific aspect of uncertainty, interaction, or complexity present in the environment. Understanding these properties helps in selecting appropriate agent architectures, decision-making strategies, and learning mechanisms.

1.5.4 Fully Observable vs. Partially Observable Environments

In a **fully observable environment**., an agent has complete access to all relevant information about the current state of the environment through its sensors. There is no hidden or missing information, allowing the agent to make decisions with certainty. In contrast, a **partially observable environment** provides incomplete or noisy information, requiring the agent to infer missing details or maintain an internal state to make rational decisions. Most real-world environments are partially observable due to sensor limitations or uncertainty.

Example: A chess-playing agent operates in a fully observable environment, while a self-driving car operates in a partially observable environment.

1.5.5 Deterministic vs. Stochastic Environments

A **deterministic environment**. is one in which the outcome of an action is completely predictable, given the current state and the action performed. There is no randomness involved. In a **stochastic environment**, actions may lead to different outcomes even under identical conditions due to uncertainty or random events. Designing agents for stochastic environments requires probabilistic reasoning and robustness.

Example: A calculator program is deterministic, whereas stock market trading operates in a stochastic environment.

1.5.6 Competitive vs. Collaborative Environments

In a **competitive environment**., multiple agents have conflicting goals, and the success of one agent may reduce the success of others. In a **collaborative environment**, agents work together toward a common goal and share information or resources. Many real-world systems involve a mix of both competition and collaboration.

Example: Chess is a competitive environment, while a team of robots assembling a product operates in a collaborative environment.

1.5.7 Single-Agent vs. Multi-Agent Environments

A **single-agent environment**. contains only one agent interacting with the environment, and the agent's performance depends solely on its own actions. In a **multi-agent environment**, multiple agents coexist and interact, and their actions may affect each other's outcomes. Such environments require coordination, negotiation, or strategic reasoning.

Example: A personal recommendation system is a single-agent environment, whereas traffic control systems involve multiple agents (vehicles).

1.5.8 Static vs. Dynamic Environments

In a **static environment**., the environment does not change while the agent is making a decision. In a **dynamic environment**, changes may occur independently of the agent's actions, requiring continuous sensing and rapid response. Dynamic environments demand real-time decision-making and adaptability.

Example: Solving a crossword puzzle is static, while driving a vehicle in traffic is dynamic.

1.5.9 Discrete vs. Continuous Environments

A **discrete environment**. has a finite or countable number of states, actions, or time steps. In contrast, a **continuous environment** involves continuous ranges of values, such as speed, temperature, or time. Continuous environments are more complex and often require mathematical modelling and approximation techniques.

Example: Chess is a discrete environment, while robotic arm movement in space is a continuous environment.

1.5.10 Episodic vs. Sequential Environments

In an **episodic environment**., the agent's experience is divided into independent episodes, and actions in one episode do not affect future episodes. In a **sequential environment**, current actions influence future states and decisions, requiring planning and foresight.

Example: An image classification system is episodic, while a game-playing agent operates in a sequential environment.

1.5.11 Known vs. Unknown Environments

A **known environment**. is one where the agent has complete knowledge of the environment's rules, dynamics, and outcomes. In an **unknown environment**, the agent must learn how the environment works through exploration and experience. Learning agents are particularly useful in unknown environments.

Example: A programmed board game is a known environment, whereas an exploration robot on Mars faces an unknown environment.

1.5.12 Accessible vs. Inaccessible Environments

An **accessible environment**. allows the agent to obtain all necessary information about the environment's state through its sensors. In an **inaccessible environment**, some information cannot be directly perceived, making decision-making more difficult. Agents must rely on estimation or prediction in such cases.

Example: A temperature-controlled room is accessible, while underwater exploration with limited sensors is inaccessible.

1.5.13 Benign vs. Adversarial Environments

A **benign environment**. does not actively attempt to harm or obstruct the agent, and any uncertainty is due to natural causes. An **adversarial environment** contains entities that deliberately work against the agent's objectives. Such environments require strategic reasoning and often involve game-theoretic approaches.

Example: A weather prediction system operates in a benign environment, while cybersecurity systems operate in adversarial environments.

1.6 The Structure of Agents.

The **structure of an intelligent agent** describes how an agent is internally organized to perceive its environment., make decisions, and perform actions. At a fundamental level, an agent consists of a **physical or software-based body**, sensors to perceive the environment, actuators to act upon it, and an internal decision-making mechanism called the **agent program**. Together, these components enable the agent to function autonomously and rationally within a given task environment.

Agent = Architecture + Agent Program

The **architecture**. provides the hardware or software platform on which the agent operates, such as a computer system, robot body, or embedded controller. The **agent program** runs on this architecture and maps percept sequences (inputs from sensors) to actions (outputs to actuators). Different architectures support different levels of intelligence., ranging from simple rule-based systems to advanced learning-based agents.

1.6.1 Sensors. and Actuators.

Sensors. allow the agent to perceive its environment.. These may include physical sensors such as cameras, microphones, temperature sensors, or virtual sensors such as keyboard input, web APIs, and data streams. The collection of all percepts over time is known as the **percept sequence**, which forms the basis for decision-making.

Actuators. enable the agent to act upon the environment.. In physical agents, actuators include motors, wheels, robotic arms, or speakers. In software agents, actuators may include displaying text, sending messages, executing commands, or placing transactions. The effectiveness of an agent depends on how well its actuators allow it to influence the environment.

1.6.2 Agent Program (Decision-Making Component)

The **agent program** is the core of the agent's intelligence. It processes percepts received from sensors and determines the appropriate action. Depending on the agent type, this program may be implemented using condition–action rules (simple reflex agents), internal state models (model-based agents), goal reasoning and planning (goal-based agents), utility. .maximization (utility-based agents), or learning algorithms (learning agents).

1.6.3 Internal State and Knowledge Base

More advanced agents maintain an **internal state** that represents aspects of the environment. not directly observable through sensors. This internal state is updated using percepts and prior knowledge. A **knowledge base** may store facts, rules, models, or learned experiences that help the agent reason about the world. This enables agents to operate effectively in partially observable and dynamic environments.

1.6.4 Learning Component (Optional but Advanced)

In learning agents, the structure includes additional components such as a **learning element**, **critic**, and **problem generator**. These components allow the agent to improve its performance over time by learning from feedback and experience. Learning enables adaptation, autonomy, and improved rationality., especially in complex and uncertain environments.

1.6.5 Interaction with the Environment

The agent operates in a continuous loop known as the perception–decision–action cycle. It perceives the environment. through sensors, processes this information using the agent program and internal state, and then acts using actuators. This interaction continues until the task is completed or the agent is terminated.

1.7 Types of Agents

Agents form the core concept of Artificial Intelligence, as they provide a unified way to describe intelligent behaviour. Any entity that employs sensors to perceive the environment. and actuators to act upon them in order to accomplish set objectives qualifies as an agent. It is possible to understand complex intelligent behaviour in terms of perception, decision-making, and action by modelling AI systems as agents. AI researchers may create, evaluate, and contrast various intelligent systems in a methodical and organized way thanks to this agent-based approach. Figure 1.9, illustrates the major types of AI agents used in artificial intelligence. systems.

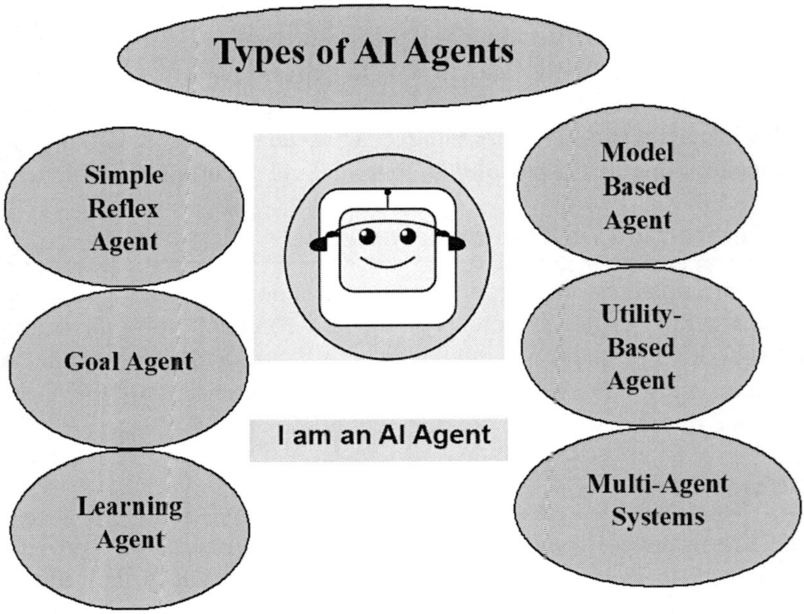

Figure 1.9 Types of AI Agents

1.7.1 Simple Reflex Agents

Simple reflex agents are the most basic form of intelligent agents. These agents operate using a set of predefined condition–action rules, where specific percepts directly trigger specific actions. They do not maintain any internal memory of past events and do not learn from experience. Because of this, simple reflex agents are effective only in static and fully observable environments, where the current percept is sufficient to determine the correct action. The structure of a simple reflex agent is illustrated in Figure 1.10.

A simple reflex agent responds immediately to the current state of the environment without considering previous states or future consequences. Since these agents lack memory and learning capability, they fail in dynamic or complex environments where decision-making requires historical context or adaptation. Despite their limitations, simple reflex agents are widely used in applications where fast and straightforward responses are required.

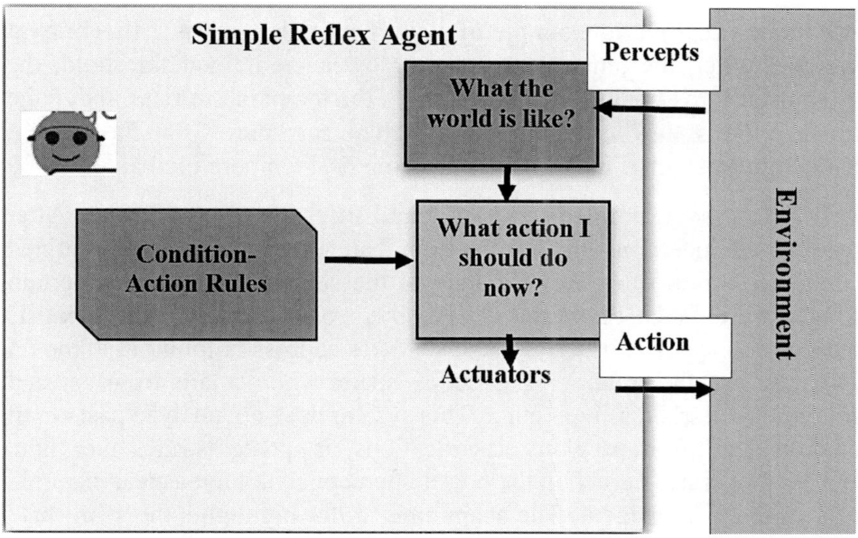

Figure 1.10 Simple Reflex Agent.

A simple reflex agent makes decisions solely on the current percept **without considering internal state or past actions.**

Agent ⟶ Sensor ⟶ Environment ⟶ Actuators

"What the world is like now?" → Condition–Action Rules → "What action I should do now"

Agent's program is based on: Condition–Action Rules, which specify actions to be taken based on certain conditions being met.

Examples of Simple Reflex Agents: Examples of simple reflex agents are:

1. Automatic hand sanitizer dispenser
2. Motion-activated lights
3. Thermostat
4. Smoke detectors

A common real-world example of a simple reflex agent is a **thermostat system**. When the temperature falls below a predefined threshold, the thermostat turns the heater on, and when the temperature rises above the limit, it turns the heater off. The system acts purely on the current temperature reading, without remembering past temperature values.

Another classic example is a **spam email filter** based on fid rules. After reading an incoming email, the filter categorizes it using predefined condition–action rules. For instance, if the subject line contains certain trigger words such as *"free," "buy now,"* or *"discount,"* the email is marked *as spam. Similarly, if the sender's address is found in a known spammer list, the email is classified as spam, while emails from verified sources are marked as non-spam. This system does not analyze past email patterns, learn from previous classifications, or update its rules over time. Hence, it operates purely on the present percept, making it a clear example of a simple reflex agent. The spam email filter highlights the **stimulus–response mechanism** of reflex-based AI systems While such systems are efficient and fast for simple tasks, they are limited in handling complex, evolving, or context-dependent scenarios.

1.7.2 Model-Based Reflex Agents

Model-based reflex agents represent advancement over simple reflex agents by maintaining an **internal model of the environment**. This internal model allows the agent to keep track of changes in the environment over time, making it suitable for **partially observable and dynamic environments**. The architecture. of a model-based reflex agent is shown in Figure 1.11.

Unlike simple reflex agents, model-based agents use past percepts along with current sensory input to update their internal state. They rely on two important models: a **world model**, which describes how the environment. behaves, and a **transition model**, which predicts how the environment changes in response to the agent's actions. By combining these models, the agent can make more informed decisions.

The **state tracker** is a key component of a model-based agent. It maintains the agent's current understanding of the world by integrating new percepts with previous information. The world model defines how the environment. evolves, while the transition model helps predict the outcomes of possible actions. This capability enables the agent to anticipate future states and select appropriate actions even when all information is not directly observable.

The operation of a model-based agent involves three main phases. In the **perception phase**, sensory input is received and used to update the internal state. In the **state update phase**, new data is combined with prior knowledge to maintain a consistent representation of the environment.. Finally, in the **action selection phase**, the agent evaluates different actions using the transition model and selects the most suitable action based on predicted outcomes.

Model-based agents offer several advantages over simple reflex agents. They provide **enhanced decision-making**, better handling of partial observability, and improved prediction capabilities. These agents can adapt to changing environments by updating their internal models and learning from experience. A practical example of a model-based agent is **autonomous vehicle navigation**, where the vehicle continuously updates its understanding of the surroundings and predicts the effects of its actions to navigate safely.

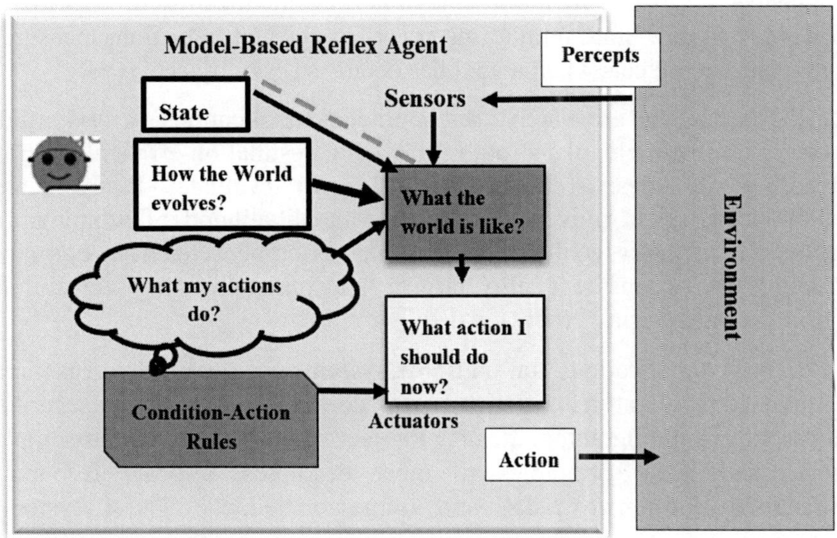

Figure 1.11 Model-Based Reflex Agent.

1.7.3 Goal-Based Agents

Goal-based agents are intelligent systems that select their actions by considering how well those actions help achieve specific objectives. Unlike simple or model-based reflex agents that react immediately to current perceptions, goal-based agents evaluate possible future states of the environment. By reasoning about the consequences of their actions, these agents demonstrate greater flexibility and intelligence, making them suitable for complex and dynamic problem-solving tasks.

At the core of a goal-based agent is an explicit representation of goals that define the desired outcomes. These goals guide the agent's behaviour and provide a clear purpose for decision-making. The agent continuously assesses whether its current state is moving closer to or farther from the goal. This capability allows the agent to plan ahead, compare alternative actions, and choose the sequence of steps that best leads to goal achievement.

The architecture of a goal-based agent typically includes a **goal formulation module**, a **planning system**, and a **state monitoring mechanism**. The goal formulation module defines and manages objectives, often organizing them into a hierarchy based on priority or importance. The planning system generates and evaluates possible action sequences, predicting their outcomes and selecting the most effective path toward the goal. State monitoring tracks the current situation, measures progress, and detects when a goal has been successfully achieved.

Goal-based agents are widely used in practical applications. A **navigation system**, for example, plans routes to reach a destination efficiently while avoiding obstacles. A **chess-playing agent** evaluates future board positions to select moves that increase the likelihood of winning. In **industrial robotics**, goal-based agents plan assembly sequences, optimize resource usage, ensure quality targets, and maintain safety constraints during manufacturing processes.

In everyday applications, **smart home systems** use goal-based reasoning to manage temperature, optimize energy consumption, maintain security, and control lighting automatically. **Project management systems** apply goal-based agent principles to meet deadlines, allocate resources effectively, minimize risks, and optimize budgets. These systems demonstrate how goal-driven decision-making improves efficiency and reliability in real-world environments.

Advanced implementations of goal-based agents often use **hierarchical goal structures**, where complex goals are broken down into smaller sub-goals. They may also support **dynamic goal adjustment**, allowing the agent to modify objectives in response to changing environmental conditions. Performance is evaluated using metrics such as goal achievement rate, resource utilization, planning time, and adaptation speed.

Despite their advantages, goal-based agents face challenges such as resolving conflicting goals, managing limited resources, handling uncertainty, and performing real-time planning. Common solution approaches include priority-based goal selection, resource-aware planning, probabilistic evaluation of outcomes, and incremental planning techniques.

Future developments in goal-based agents focus on integrating machine learning to improve goal reasoning, enhancing planning efficiency, handling uncertainty more effectively, and coordinating goals across multiple agents. Ongoing research aims to develop agents capable of real-time replanning, advanced goal learning, and seamless collaboration in complex, multi-agent environments.

1.7.4 Utility-Based Agents

Utility-based agents represent an advanced class of intelligent agents that go beyond merely achieving goals by evaluating how *desirable* different outcomes are. Instead of checking whether a goal is reached or not, these agents use a **utility function** to assign a numerical value to each possible outcome. The agent then selects the action that **maximizes overall utility**, making this approach especially useful in situations where multiple possible solutions exist and trade-offs must be considered. Figure 1.12 illustrates the structure of utility-based agent

The concept of **utility** originates from economics, where it refers to the satisfaction or value gained from a product or service. In artificial intelligence, utility is used to quantify how well a particular state of the environment. satisfies the agent's preferences. Unlike goal-based agents that treat all goal-achieving states as equally good, utility-based agents compare outcomes and choose the best among them. For example, a self-driving car may evaluate different routes by considering safety, travel time, fuel efficiency, and comfort, and then select the route with the highest overall utility. This ability makes utility-based agents more flexible, adaptive, and robust in complex and uncertain environments.

The Rationale Behind the Usage of "Utility": Goals only offer a binary choice of outcomes; they can be either achieved or not (e.g., happy vs. sad). However, rather than a straightforward yes/no choice, many real-life situations involve degrees of preferences/choices-goals. The idea of utility, which gives outcomes a numerical value and enables systems to assess options and select the one that offers the highest overall satisfaction or benefit, is used by economists and computer scientists to capture this.

Utility functions in AI enable agents to assess different/multiple states and activities on a continuous scale. This increases the flexibility and rationality. of decision-making, particularly when there are trade-offs between conflicting goals like comfort, safety, cost, and time.

A utility.-based agent consists of several key architectural components. The **utility function** defines preferences by assigning numerical values to different states of the environment. The **state evaluation system** interprets the current situation in terms of utility and guides decision-making. Using sensors, the agent perceives the environment and predicts the possible outcomes of available actions. These predicted outcomes are then evaluated using the utility function, and the agent selects the action that yields the maximum expected utility.

The decision-making process of a utility-based agent typically involves four steps. First, the agent perceives the current state of the environment.. Next, it predicts the possible results of different actions. Then, it calculates the utility values of these predicted outcomes. Finally, it chooses the action that maximizes the utility. This systematic process enables the agent to handle uncertainty and conflicting objectives more effectively than simpler agent models.

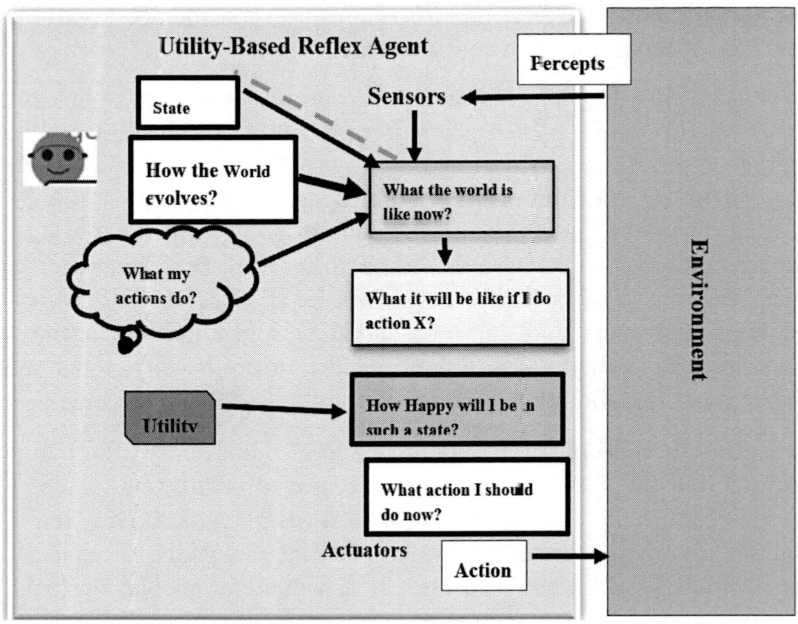

Figure 1.12 Utility-Based Reflex Agent

Utility-based agents are widely used in real-world applications. In **investment portfolio management**, such agents analyze market conditions, predict future returns, and select portfolios that maximize expected profit while managing risk. In **healthcare systems**, utility-based decision support tools help optimize treatment plans, allocate resources efficiently, and assess patient risks. **Energy management systems**, such as smart grids, use utility functions to balance load, minimize costs, and reduce environmental impact. Similarly, **financial trading systems** employ utility-based strategies for asset allocation, risk management, and market timing.

Advanced utility.-based systems rely on **multi-attribute utility theory**, where multiple factors are considered simultaneously. Modern AI systems can also **learn utility functions** using techniques such as inverse reinforcement learning, preference learning, and experience-based adaptation. Optimization techniques like heuristic search, Monte Carlo simulations, and parameter tuning are used to improve decision strategies and computational efficiency. As AI continues to evolve, utility-based agents are expected to play a critical role in building intelligent systems capable of making balanced, rational, and context-aware decisions.

1.7.5 Learning Agents

Learning agents are the most advanced type of intelligent agents, distinguished by their ability to improve their performance over time by learning from experience. Unlike simple, model-based, goal-based, or utility.-based agents, learning agents are not limited to fid rules or predefined models. Instead, they continuously adapt their behaviour based on feedback from the environment. This makes learning agents particularly suitable for dynamic, uncertain, and complex environments where conditions change and prior knowledge may be incomplete.

The **architecture of a learning agent**, as illustrated in Figure 1.13, consists of four main components that work together to enable adaptation and improvement. The **performance element** is responsible for selecting and executing actions in the environment. using the agent's current knowledge and learned policies. It directly interacts with the environment through sensors and actuators. The **learning element** improves the performance element by modifying its knowledge base and decision-making rules based on experience. It identifies areas where performance can be enhanced and updates behaviour accordingly.

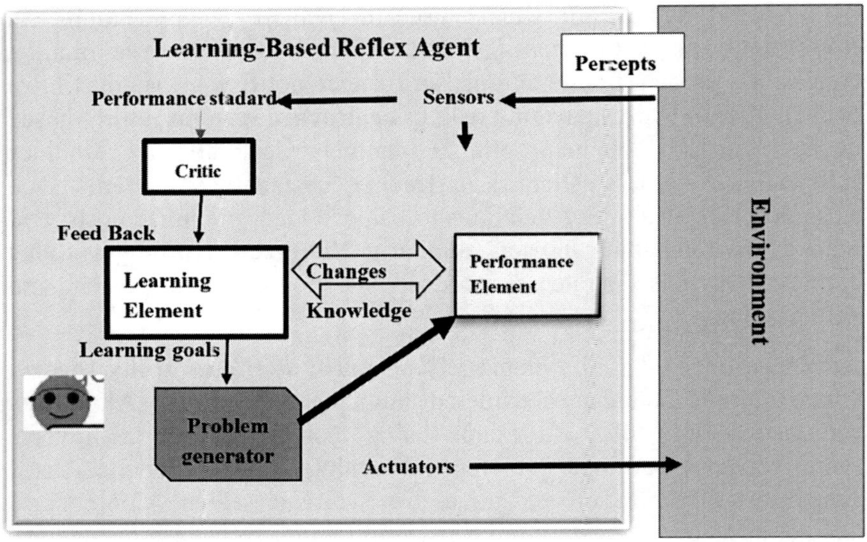

Figure1.13 Learning Agent

1.7.5.1 Conceptual Components of a Learning Agent

1. **Learning Element**
   - Responsible for making improvements.

2. **Performance Element**
   - Responsible for selecting external actions.

3. **Critic**
   - Gives feedback based on how the agent is doing.
   - Determines how good the performance is and whether the performance element should be modified for improved future decisions.

4. **Problem Generator**
   - Responsible for suggesting actions that will lead to new, informative experiences.
   - Its job is to **suggest exploratory actions**.

- The **critic** evaluates the agent's actions by comparing the outcomes with a desired performance standard. It provides feedback on how well the agent is performing and generates learning signals that guide improvement. Complementing this, the **problem generator** encourages exploration by suggesting new or less-tried actions. It helps manage the exploration–exploitation trade-off, ensuring that the agent not only uses known successful strategies but also explores new possibilities that may lead to better performance in the future.

Examples of Learning Agents

1. **Reinforcement Learning Agents**
   - AlphaGo
   - OpenAI-5
2. **Natural Language Processing Agents**
   - GPT-3
   - GPT-4
   - BERT
   - (Bidirectional Encoder Representations from Transformers)
3. **Autonomous Vehicles**
   - Wymo
   - Tesla Autopilot
4. **Robotics**
   - Boston Dynamics
   - Robotic Arm Manipulators
5. **Game Playing**
6. **Recommender Systems**
   - Learning agents employ different **learning mechanisms** depending on the nature of the task.

In **supervised learning**, the agent learns from labelled examples and is commonly used in classification and regression problems.

Reinforcement learning allows the agent to learn through interaction with the environment using reward-based feedback, making it highly effective for sequential decision-making tasks such as games and robotics.

Unsupervised learning helps the agent discover patterns, structures, and features in data without explicit labels, supporting tasks like clustering and dimensionality reduction.

Learning agents are widely used in real-world applications. In **game playing**, the power chess engines, Go players, and strategy-based games. In **robotics**, learning agents enable motion learning, task adaptation, manipulation, and navigation in changing environments. In **natural language processing**, they support language understanding, machine translation, dialogue systems, and sentiment analysis by learning from large volumes of textual data.

Different **learning strategies** are adopted based on application requirements. (1) **Online learning** allows agents to update knowledge continuously in real time, (2) **batch learning** processes accumulated experience periodically for stable improvement, and (3) **Transfer learning** enables agents to reuse knowledge gained in one task or domain to improve performance in another, reducing training time and data requirements.

The performance of learning agents is evaluated using metrics such as learning rate, convergence speed, resource utilization, adaptability, robustness, and generalization ability. However, implementing learning agents also presents challenges, including catastrophic forgetting, sample inefficiency, balancing exploration and exploitation, and scalability in real-world environments. These challenges are addressed using techniques such as experience replay, adaptive exploration strategies, hybrid learning architectures, and distributed learning systems.

Future developments in learning agents focus on advanced learning methods such as meta-learning, few-shot learning, and self-supervised learning. Emerging architectures emphasize modular, hierarchical, and multi-agent learning frameworks. Learning agents are expected to play a crucial role in future applications including autonomous systems, healthcare diagnostics, smart cities, financial systems, and environmental monitoring.

1.7.6 Multi-Agent Systems

A **Multi-Agent System (MAS)** consists of multiple intelligent agents that interact with one another within a shared environment. to achieve individual or collective goals. Unlike single-agent systems, multi-agent systems emphasize cooperation, coordination, and sometimes competition among agents. Each agent in the system operates autonomously, making its own decisions while considering the presence and actions of other agents. MAS are widely used in distributed problem-solving, simulations, robotics, and large-scale real-world systems where a single agent cannot efficiently solve the problem alone.

One of the key characteristics of multi-agent systems is **autonomy**, where each agent independently controls its behaviour and manages local objectives. Agents also possess **social ability**, enabling them to communicate, negotiate, and coordinate with other agents using defined protocols. Additionally, agents are **reactive**, meaning they can perceive and respond to environmental changes in real time, and **proactive**, as they take initiative by setting goals and anticipating future situations rather than merely reacting to events.

The architecture. of a multi-agent system includes a **communication infrastructure** that allows agents to exchange messages and share information efficiently. **Coordination mechanisms** play a vital role in allocating tasks, sharing resources, and resolving conflicts among agents. MAS can adopt different organizational structures, such as hierarchical systems with centralized control, peer-to-peer systems with equal agents, or hybrid structures that combine both approaches. Interaction among agents follows specific protocols for cooperation, negotiation, and conflict resolution to ensure smooth system functioning.

Multi-agent systems are used in a wide range of applications. In **distributed problem solving**, MAS are applied in traffic management, search and rescue operations, power grid control, and supply chain optimization. In **simulation and modelling**, they are used to study social behaviour, economic markets, and ecological systems. Industrial applications include manufacturing automation, logistics management, and quality control. Coordination in MAS may be **centralized**, **decentralized**, or **hybrid**, depending on system requirements and scalability needs.

Learning also plays an important role in multi-agent systems. Agents may engage in **collaborative learning**, where they share experiences and knowledge, or **competitive learning**, where agents adapt strategies in adversarial or market-based environments. Performance of MAS is evaluated using metrics such as scalability, robustness, efficiency, and adaptability. However, challenges such as coordination overhead, communication reliability, and resource conflicts must be addressed through adaptive coordination strategies, reliable communication protocols, and well-designed organizational structures. Future directions in multi-agent systems include integration with emerging technologies such as block chain, cloud computing, and edge AI. Applications are expanding into smart cities, autonomous vehicle fleets, healthcare systems, and environmental monitoring. Ongoing research focuses on swarm intelligence, emergent behaviour, trust mechanisms, and social learning, making multi-agent systems a crucial area of modern artificial intelligence research. Figure 1.14 depicts the architecture of Multi-Agent System (MAS).

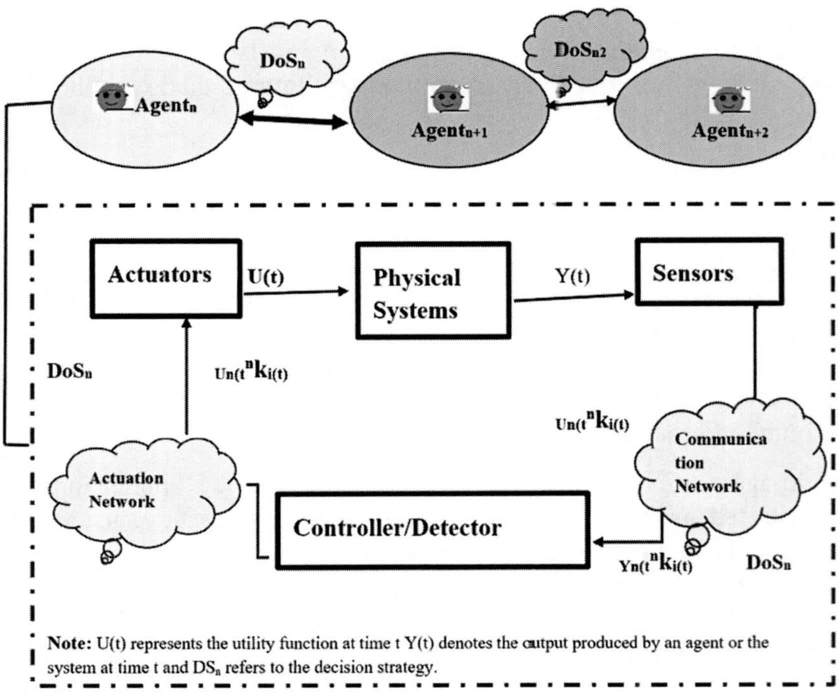

Figure 1.14 Multi-Agent Systems

Chapter 1: Summary

This chapter introduced the foundational concepts of **Artificial Intelligence (AI)** by addressing the fundamental question: *What is Artificial Intelligence?* AI was presented as a field concerned with designing systems capable of perceiving their environment, reasoning with available information, and acting intelligently to achieve specific goals. The chapter highlighted multiple perspectives of AI—thinking and acting humanly, as well as thinking and acting rationally—emphasizing rational behaviour as the central theme of modern AI systems.

The **foundations and history of AI** were discussed to provide context for the evolution of the field. Beginning with early theoretical contributions and landmark events such as the Dartmouth Conference, the chapter traced AI's progress through symbolic approaches, expert systems, periods of reduced funding, and the eventual resurgence driven by machine learning and data-driven techniques. This historical overview helped students understand how AI has matured from theoretical concepts into practical technologies used in real-world applications.

A significant portion of the chapter focused on **intelligent agents**, which serve as the core abstraction in AI. Agents were defined as entities that perceive through sensors and act through actuators. Different **types of agents**—simple reflex, model-based, goal-based, utility-based, learning agents, and multi-agent systems—were explained to show increasing levels of intelligence, adaptability, and autonomy. The interaction between agents and their **environments** was emphasized as a key determinant of agent behaviour and design.

The chapter also examined the **concept of rationality**, clarifying that a rational agent is one that selects actions expected to maximize its performance measure, given its percept sequence and knowledge. Rationality was shown to depend on factors such as available information, learning ability, and autonomy, rather than on omniscience or perfection. This led naturally to a discussion on the **nature of environments**, where environments were classified along multiple dimensions such as observability, determinism, episodic vs. sequential behaviour, and adversarial conditions.

Finally, the chapter explained the **structure of agents**, outlining how an agent's architecture. and agent program work together to produce intelligent behaviour. By understanding how perception, internal processing, and action selection are organized, students gain insight into how abstract AI concepts are implemented in practical systems.

Conclusions

Chapter 1 establishes a strong conceptual foundation for Artificial Intelligence by unifying diverse ideas under the agent-based view of intelligence. By modelling AI systems as rational agents operating within specific environments, the chapter provides a coherent framework for understanding how intelligent behaviour emerges from perception, reasoning, and action.

The discussions on rationality and environment classification emphasize that intelligence is not absolute but context-dependent. An agent's effectiveness depends on how well it is designed for its task environment and how appropriately it balances knowledge, learning, and autonomy. Understanding these principles is essential before studying advanced topics such as problem-solving, search techniques, and learning algorithms.

Overall, this chapter prepares students to think systematically about AI systems and sets the stage for subsequent chapters that explore problem-solving agents, search strategies, and learning methods in greater depth. The concepts introduced here serve as the intellectual building blocks for the entire study of Artificial Intelligence.

Chapter – 2

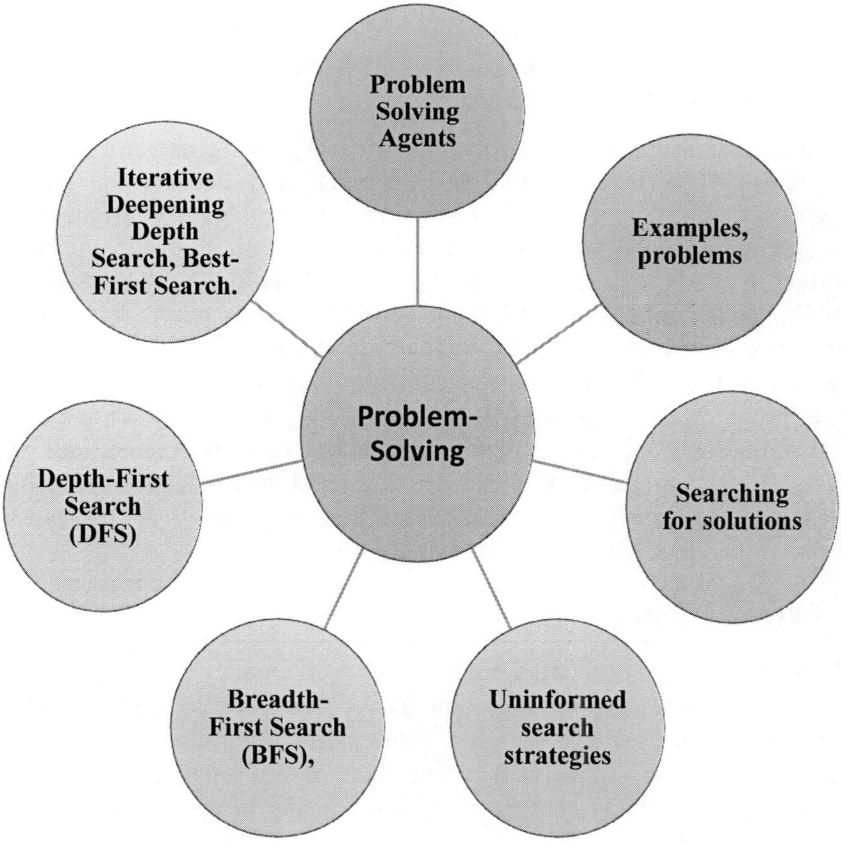
Problem-Solving
Problem Solving Agents
Examples, problems
Searching for solutions
Uninformed search strategies
Breadth-First Search (BFS),
Depth-First Search (DFS)
Iterative Deepening Depth Search, Best-First Search.

Introduction to Problem Solving

At the heart of artificial intelligence lies problem-solving, where intelligent agents have to Figure out how to go from an initial state to a desired goal state. Many AI applications, like playing, route planning, scheduling, and automated reasoning, require the agent to explore a structured problem space as opposed to have a quick fix. For these kinds of problem-solving agents, search techniques are essential tools that allow them to systematically investigate possible states and make choices within constraints. An AI system can analyze the environment, assess possible courses of action, and find solutions through search—even in difficult and unknown/unfamiliar domains areas.

Thus, search is an essential concept in artificial intelligence, providing as the basis for efficient planning, reasoning, and decision-making. It involves examining or exploring several problem states or configurations in order achieve a specific goal or objective. Search algorithms provide formal methods for addressing challenges such as finding optimal paths, solving constraint-based puzzles, and generating action plans. This chapter provides basic search methods, such as Breadth-First Search, Depth-First Search, and Iterative Deepening Depth-First Search, with an emphasis on uninformed search strategies. It also introduces problem-solving agents and formulates example situations. Learners can understand how AI systems efficiently explore problem spaces and how various approaches influence performance, completeness, and optimality in real-world problem-solving situations by studying these strategies.

2.1 Problem Solving Agents

Problem-solving agents are systems which meticulously evaluate possible actions and states for solving complex problems. These agents employ structured strategies like search algorithms, heuristics, and methods of optimization to accomplish their goals. Examples of route planning agents in navigation systems and puzzle-solving agents in games demonstrate how these agents operate in real-world and abstract domains, respectively. By utilizing suitable search strategies, these agents can efficiently find optimal or near-optimal solutions to challenging problems. Problem-solving agents are fundamental to Artificial Intelligence (AI) as they provide a framework for designing systems that can make decisions and solve problems.

2.1.1 Definition of Problem-Solving Agents

A problem-solving agent is an **AI system that decides what actions to take in order to achieve a specific goal**. These agents use a variety of techniques to explore and navigate through a **problem space**, which is a representation of all possible states and actions.

2.1.2 Key Characteristics of Problem-Solving Agents

a) **Goal-Driven Behaviour**: Problem-solving agents are driven by specific goals, navigating a defined state space to achieve desired outcomes.

b) **State Space Representation**: Problems are modelled as states and actions, where each state represents a configuration of the environment, and actions define transitions between states.

c) **Search Strategies**: Agents employ to explore the state space. These can be:

d) **Uninformed Search**: Lacking additional information about the goal.

e) **Informed Search**: Guided by to improve efficiency.

2.1.3 Components of a Problem-Solving Agent

a) **Goal Formulation**

- The agent decides the goal based on the given problem. Goal formulation is the process in which the agent defines what it wants to achieve. The goal is the desired state that the agent ais to reach.

b) **Problem Formulation the Agent Must Define the Problem By:**

- Starting from the initial state
- Identifying the set of possible actions
- Considering the environment and constraints Problem formulation helps the agent understand what must be solved and how to proceed.

c) **Search Strategy**

- The agent uses a search strategy to find the best path to reach the goal state. Search strategies decide the order in which actions are applied in exploring different states to form a path toward the goal.

d) Execution

- Execution involves carrying out the solution derived by the search strategy to achieve the goal. The agent performs a sequence of actions that lead to the desired goal state.

2.1.4 Steps in Problem-Solving (7 Processes)

a) **Initial State**: The starting point of the problem. It is the situation from which the agent begins the search.

b) **Actions**: Actions define what the agent can take from one state to the next. Each action transforms the current state into a different state.

c) **Transition Model**: The transition model defines the outcome of each action. It describes what state results from performing a particular action.

d) **Goal Test**: The goal test is a function that checks whether a given state is a goal state or not. It determines if the current state satisfies the goal condition.

e) **Path Cost**: The path cost is a numeric value (a function) that assigns a cost to a path. It helps in evaluating the efficiency of the solution.

f) **Solution**: A solution is an action sequence that leads from the initial state to the goal state.

g) **Optimal Solution**: An optimal solution is the solution with the lowest cost among all possible solutions. It represents the minimum cost path.

2.1.5 Components of a Problem-Solving Agent.

To operate effectively, problem-solving agents rely on the following components:

To operate effectively, problem-solving agents rely on the following components:

- **State Space Representation**: A model of all possible states and actions in the environment.
- **Initial State**: The starting configuration of the problem.
- **Goal Test**: A condition to determine if the goal state is reached.

- **Action Set**: The set of possible actions available to the agent.
- **Transition Model**: Rules that define how actions transform states.
- **Path Cost Function**: A measure of the cost associated with a sequence of Path Cost.

By combining these characteristics and components, problem-solving agents systematically explore their environment to identify and execution solutions, making them essential tools in for addressing a wide range of decision-making and planning tasks.

2.2 Properties of Search Algorithms

Following are the four essential properties of search algorithms to compare the efficiency of these algorithms:

1. **Completeness**
    - If a search algorithm is **complete**, it means that if a solution to the search problem exists, the algorithm is **guaranteed to find a solution** and return a solution **at any point** during its search.
    - Solution exists for any random input.
2. **Optimality**
    - If a solution is found, then the algorithm is **optimal** if the best solution (**Lowest Path Cost**) among all others (solutions) is returned.
    - The best solution here is related to the path cost.
    - If the search algorithm is guaranteed to return the best solution, then such a solution is said to be an **Optimal Solution**.
3. **Time Complexity**
    - Time complexity is a measure of the **time** taken by an algorithm (search) to complete the task.
    - This is the maximum time complexity of the algorithm.
4. **Space Complexity**
    - Space complexity is a measure of the **storage space** required by an algorithm at any point during the search process.
    - This is the maximum space complexity of the algorithm.

2.2 Example Problems

Problem solving agents are commonly used in both theoretical and real-world/practical contexts. A typical example is a route-planning agent found in GPS applications and other navigation systems. The agent formulates the problem by /formulating/evaluating possible routes, intersections, and road conditions given a starting point and a destination. After that, it looks for the shortest or most efficient means for reaching there.

Another example would be an agent that solves puzzles, such the 8-puzzle or 15-puzzle problems. In this case, the starting state is denoted by the initial tile arrangement, and the goal is to arrive at a particular target configuration. Using search algorithms, the agent investigates several move sequences until it discovers one that results in the goal state.

Game-playing agents, like those seen in board games like tic tac toe or chess, can also solve problems. The agent chooses actions that improve the chances of winning after taking into account possible moves and assessing potential game states. Although games may involve additional elements such as competition and strategy, the underlying process is still based on problem formulation and search.

These examples illustrate how problem-solving agents apply search techniques to move from an initial state to a goal state. Understanding these agents helps students grasp how Artificial Intelligence systems reason, plan, and solve problems in a systematic manner.

2.3 Searching for Solutions and Search Strategies

"Search strategies are fundamental tools for problem-solving agents

in Artificial Intelligence, enabling them to navigate complex decision-making scenarios and find solutions in problem spaces using both uninformed and informed approaches their applications in solving real-world problems."

Search is an essential concept in Artificial Intelligence (AI), laying the foundation for strategies for solving problems required to navigate complex decision-making environments. It comprises specifically exploring a variety of different states or configurations with the aim achieve a specific objective/goal. Search algorithms provide the structure for tackling a number of challenges, such finding the shortest path in a network, solving puzzles, and planning activities. This chapter covers some search strategies, both uninformed and informed, and illustrates how

AI systems employ these approaches to identify efficient solutions. Presented are the principles that allow AI to reason, plan, and act effectively in a broad spectrum of problem domains through real-world examples and clear explanations.

The simplest agents discussed in Chapter 1 were reflex agents, which select actions based on a direct mapping from percepts or states to actions. While such agents are effective in simple and fully observable environments, they perform poorly in complex domains where the number of possible states is large, making the mapping difficult to store and time-consuming to learn. In contrast, goal-based agents reason about future states and evaluate actions based on their ability to achieve desired goals. Chapter 1 introduced both simple reflex agents and goal-based agents, laying the foundation for understanding how intelligent agents progress from reactive behaviour to deliberate, goal-oriented problem solving. However, once goals are explicitly defined, an agent must determine ***how*** to achieve them. This requirement leads naturally to problem-solving agents, which employ search strategies to explore possible sequences of actions and identify paths from an initial state to a goal state. Chapter 2 focuses on these search-based approaches, explaining how intelligent agents systematically navigate problem spaces to arrive at effective solutions.

It is important to distinguish between goal and a problem. P**roblem-solving agents**, the terms have distinct roles:

Goal

- A **goal** specifies *what* the agent wants to achieve.
- It defines a **desired state or set of states**.
- **Example**: *Reach city B from city A.*

Problem

- A **problem** is a **formalized representation** of the task of achieving the goal.
- It defines *how* the goal can be achieved.
- **A problem consists of:**
  1. Initial state
  2. Actions (or operators)
  3. Transition model

4. Goal test
5. Path cost (optional)

2.4 Types of Search Algorithms

Based on the search problems, search algorithms are classified into two categories:

1. **Uninformed Search (Blind Search) Algorithms**
2. **Informed Search (Heuristic Search) Algorithms**

Search algorithms can be broadly classified into two categories based on their approach and the information they use to navigate the problem space. Figure 2.1 presents types of algorithms in AI

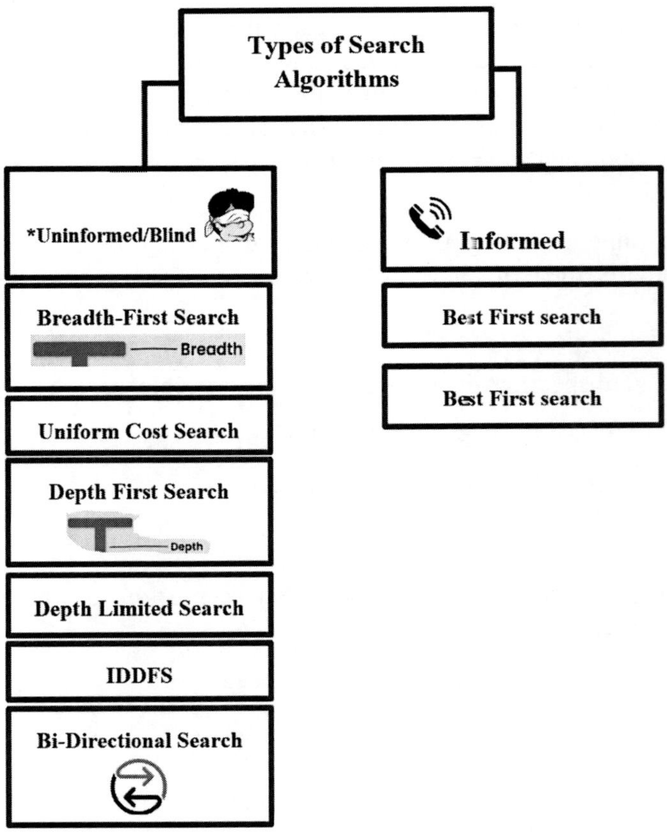

Figure 2.1 Types of Search Algorithms in AI

In this chapter we will understand the Uninformed / Blind Search, namely, the following:

1. Breadth First search,
2. Depth First Search,
3. Iterative deepening depth first search

2.4.1 Breadth First Search (BFS)

Breadth-First Search (BFS) is one of the fundamental uninformed search strategies in artificial intelligence.. It systematically expands and examines all nodes of a tree or graph structure by exploring all neighbour nodes at the present depth before moving to nodes at the next depth level.

2.4.2 A Brief Look at Bread First Search

- Breadth First Search (BFS) is a simple search strategy in which the **root node is expanded first**, then **all the successors of the root node** are expanded next, then **their successors**, and so on.
- In general **all the nodes are expanded at a given depth** in the search tree before any nodes of the next level are expanded.
- Breadth First Search is an instance of the **general graph search algorithm (**give in in the Figure 2.2) in which the shallowest unexpanded node is selected for expansion.
- This is simply achieved by using a FIFO= First in First out queue for the frontier.
- Thus, new nodes get added to the **back of the queue**, and nodes that were added earlier (and are shallower) get expanded first.
- However, it should be moved that the tweak/Twist on the general graph search algorithm is that **the goal test** is applied to each NODE when it is generated rather than when it is selected for expansion.

2.4.3 BFS Works by Following These Steps

1. Start at the root node and add it to a queue
2. Remove the first node from the queue and examine it

3. Add all unvisited neighbour nodes to the queue
4. Repeat steps 2-3 until the queue is empty or goal is found

BFS algorithm uses a First-In-First-Out (FIFO) queue data structure to maintain the frontier of nodes to be explored,

2.4.4 Properties of (BFS)

a) **Completeness:** BFS is complete, meaning it will always find a solution if one exists in a finite state space.

b) **Optimality:** When path costs are uniform, BFS is optimal as it finds the shallowest goal node first.

c) **Time Complexity:** $O(b^d)$, where b is the branching factor and d is the depth of the solution.

d) **Space Complexity:** $O(b^d)$, as it needs to store all nodes at the current level.

Figure 2.2 Illustrates the BFS Working Principle

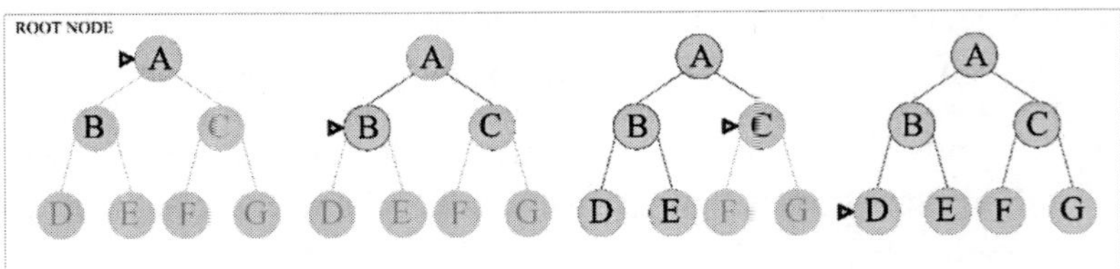

Figure 2.2 Breadth-First Search

For a Binary Tree

→ At depth **d**, the number of nodes is $\mathbf{2^d}$

→ Nodes at depth **d** = 2^d

→ Nodes at depth **d** =2^{d-1}

→ Nodes at depth **d** = =2^{d-2}

→ Nodes at d-2=2^0= 1= Goal Node

- Nodes at depth **0** = 2^{0-1}
- Nodes at depth 1=2^1= 2
- Nodes at depth 2=2^2=4
- Nodes at depth 3=2^3=8 Goal Node

Notation

$$O(2^3) = O(8) \quad \text{......................2.1}$$

2.4.5 Advantages of Breadth-First Search (BFS)

- **Complete:** BFS is guaranteed to find a solution if one exists, provided the branching factor is finite.
- **Optimal:** BFS always finds the shortest path (minimum number of steps) to the goal when all step costs are equal.
- **Systematic Exploration:** It explores nodes level by level, ensuring a structured and orderly search of the problem space.
- **Simple Implementation:** BFS is easy to understand and implement using a queue data structure.

2.4.6 Disadvantages of (BFS)

1. Memory intensive due to storing all nodes at current level
2. May be slow for very deep solutions
3. Not suitable for infinite state spaces

2.4.7 Applications of (BFS)

1. Shortest path finding in unweighted graphs
2. Web crawling
3. Social network friend suggestions
4. GPS navigation systems
5. Puzzle solving

2.4.8 Examples of (BFS)

a) **Web Crawling:** A web crawler starts from an initial URL and uses BFS to traverse the web. It visits all URLs linked from the initial pages, then visits all URLs linked from those pages, and so on.

b) **Social Network Analysis:** In social media networks, **BFS** can find the shortest path between two users recommend friends by exploring their connection of friends.

   Example: If LinkedIn uses BFS can be used to find shortest path between two professionals

c) **Routing in Networks**

d) **Solving Mazes**

e) **AI and Robotics:** In Robotics, BFS is used for path finding and navigator in an environment. Example: A robotic vacuum cleaner uses BPS.

2.5 Depth First Search (DFS)

Depth-First Search (DFS) is a prominent uninformed search technique used in AI and computer science. It investigates a problem space by going as far as possible down one branch before returning to examine other branches. DFS is particularly useful in cases where the search space is large and memory efficiency is crucial.

2.5.1 A Brief Look at Depth First Search

- Depth First Search (DFS) **always expands the deepest node in the frontier of the search** tree.
- The search proceeds immediately to the **DEEPEST LEVEL of the search tree.** Where the nodes have no successors.
- As those nodes are expanded, they are dropped from the frontier, so the search "backs up" to the next deepest mode that still has unexpanded successors.
- Depth First Search explores a graph by **selecting a path and** traversing it as deeply as possible.

2.5.2 How DFS Works?

DFS starts at the initial state (or root node) and explores a path by visiting the deepest unvisited node first. If it reaches a dead end (i.e., a state with no further unvisited neighbours or where all paths have been explored), it backtracks to the previous node and explores alternative paths. Depth first search uses a LIFO queue. A LIFO queue means that the most recently generated mode is chosen expansion.

DFS can be implemented using a stack (explicitly or via recursion). The recursive implementation is often simpler but may lead to stack overflow for very deep search spaces. This must be the deepest unexpanded mode because it is one deeper than its parents which in two was the deepest unexpected mode, when it was selected. DFS starts at the root mode, then expands all of its one branch until it reaches a dead end then BACK TRACKS to the most recent unexpanded mode, repeating until all modes are visited or specific condition is met. In simple terms DFS algorithms in AI holds the power of extending before considering the other options. Figure 2.3 illustrates the DFS working principle.

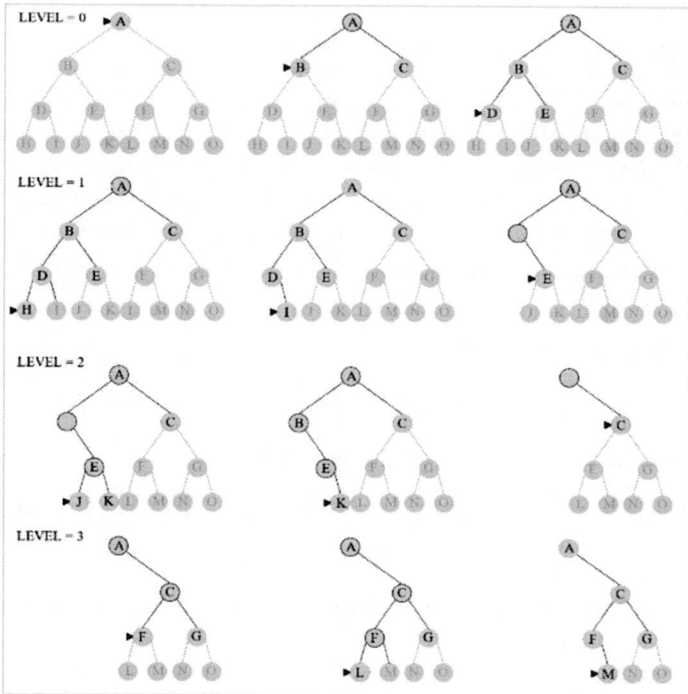

Figure 2.3 Depth First Search

2.5.3 Algorithm Steps

a) **Initialization**: Start at the initial state and push it onto a stack.

b) **Exploration**:

- ❖ Pop the top node from the stack.
- ❖ Check if it is the goal state. If yes, terminate and return the solution.
- ❖ If not, expand the node and push its unvisited neighbours onto the stack.

c) **Backtracking**: Repeat the process until the stack is empty or the goal is found.

d) **Termination**: If the stack is empty and no solution is found, conclude that no solution exists.

2.5.4 Properties of Search Algorithms

1) Completeness: DFS is complete if the graph is FINITE and the search tree has a finite depth. DFS is NOT COMPLETE in infinite-depth graphs or when it may go down a path without ever finding a solution. Depth First Search uses a LIFO (stack) structure. A LIFO queue means that the most recently generated node is selected first for expansion. This causes DFS to explore the deepest unexplored node first. It is one of the depth-oriented search in AI

When A Node is Selected?

→ DFS starts at the root node,

→ Expands the deepest unexpanded node,

→ When it reaches a dead end, DFS **backtracks** to the most recent unmet node,

→ Then continues expanding until all nodes are visited or a specific goal is found.

DFS explores as deeply as possible before considering other options.

2) Optimality

General Case: **DFS is not OPTIMAL** because it does not necessarily find the shortest or least-cost path to the goal. It explores paths to their **deepest points** before considering alternatives.

Example: In a weighted graph, DFS may find a longer or costly path first. Ignoring shorter or cheaper paths.

What is a weighted graph?

A **weighted graph** is a type of graph in which **each edge has an associated numerical value** (called weight). Figure 2.4 illustrates a weighted graph where A to E are nodes and A-B etc., are edges

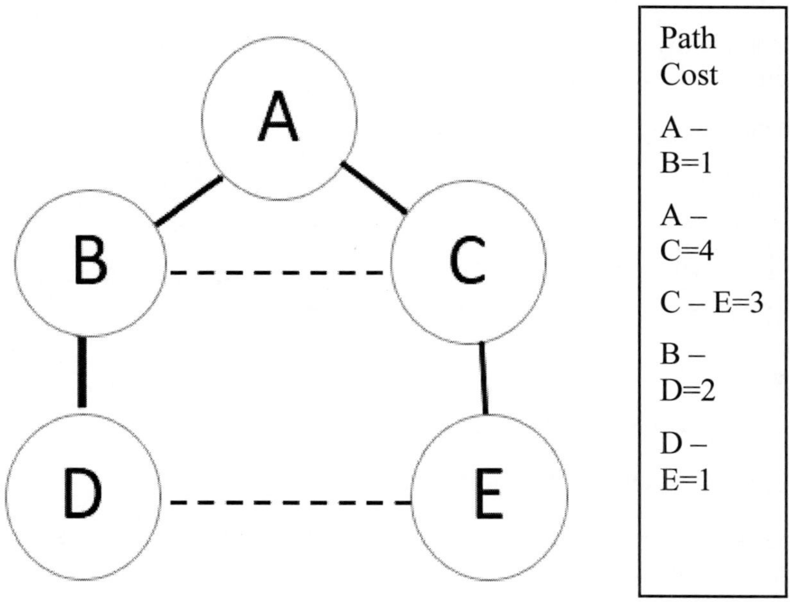

Figure 2.4 A Weighted graph

Weights can represent various metrics such as:

- Distance
- Time
- Cost
- Capacity

In this graph, finding the shortest path from **A to E** involves evaluating the weights of various paths.

- Path **A – B – D – E** has a total weight of

1 + 2 + 1 = 4

- Path **A – C – E** has a total weight of

  4 + 3 = 7

Thus, the **shortest path from A to E** is **A – B – D – E** with a **total weight of 4**.

(3) Time Complexity

Time complexity measures the amount of time an algorithm takes to complete based on the input size.

DFS Time Complexity

General Case: The time complexity of

$$\text{DFS} = O(V + E) \quad \text{......................2.2}$$

Where:

- **V** is the number of vertices
- **E** is the number of edges in the graph

Explanation: This complexity arises because DFS visits all vertices and edges in the worst case.

(4) Space Complexity

Definition: Space complexity measures the amount of memory an algorithm uses based on the input.

☆ DFS Space Complexity:

General Case:

The space complexity of **DFS** is **O(d)**, where **d** is the maximum depth of the search tree.

Explanation:

DFS requires space to store the recursion stack, which can grow up to the maximum depth of the tree.

For deeply nested trees, this can be significant.

2.5.5 Advantages of (DFS)

1. **Memory Efficiency:**
   - DFS uses memory proportional to the depth of the deepest branch being explored (O(d). [unlike Breadth-First Search (BFS), which requires storing all nodes at a level ($O(b^d)$)].
   - Ideal for problems with large state spaces and limited memory resources.
2. **Suitable for Deep Solutions:**
   - If the solution lies deep in the state space and paths are narrow, DFS can be more efficient than BFS.
3. **Easy to Implement:**
   - DFS can be implemented using either recursion or an explicit stack, making it straightforward to code.

2.5.6 Disadvantages of (DFS)

1. **Non-Optimal:**
   - DFS does not guarantee finding the shortest or least-cost solution.
   - It may explore unnecessarily deep branches, ignoring closer solutions.
2. **Completeness:**
   - DFS is not complete in infinite or cyclic state spaces unless additional mechanisms (e.g., cycle detection) are employed.
3. **Susceptible to Getting Stuck:**
   - In state spaces with infinite depth or large branching factors, DFS can get stuck exploring infinite or unproductive paths.

2.5.7 Examples of DFS in AI

1) **Path Finding (Maze):** In a maze-solving problem, DFS explores each path to its end before backtracking which cause useful for fining all possible exits.

   This approach is useful for finding all possible paths.

2) **Solving Puzzles: The 8 Puzzle**

   The **8-puzzle problem** shown in the Figure 2.5

Initial State

2	6	1
	7	8
3	4	5

Goal State

1	2	3
4	5	6
7	8	

Figure 2.5 3x3 8 puzzles

3) **Game Tree Exploration.**

   Example tu-tac-toe-chess

4) Detecting cycles in graph.

5) Topological Sorting.

2.5.8 Applications of DFS

DFS is used in various domains where memory efficiency is critical, and a solution doesn't necessarily have to be optimal. Examples include:

a) **Game Tree Exploration**: DFS is employed in exploring possible moves in games like chess.

b) **Path finding in Mazes**: Used to find a path between points in a maze or grid.

c) **Topology and Graph Algorithms**:

   ❖ **Connected Components**: Finding connected components in a graph.

- **Topological Sorting**: Ordering nodes in a directed acyclic graph.

Table 2.1 Comparison of Bidirectional DFS with Other Algorithms

Aspect	BFS	DFS
Search Space	$O(b^d)$	$O(b^d)$
Memory Efficiency	$O(b^d)$	$O(d)$
Optimality	Guaranteed for uniform-cost problems	Not guaranteed
Completeness	Guaranteed	Not guaranteed in infinite spaces

2.5.9 Variants of DFS

1. **Iterative Deepening Depth-First Search (IDDFS):**
   - Combines the space efficiency of DFS with the completeness and optimality of BFS.
   - Explores the search space iteratively with increasing depth limits.
2. **Bidirectional (DFS):**
   - Searches simultaneously from the initial state and the goal state, meeting in the middle.

DFS is an effective tool in the AI toolbox, especially when memory efficiency and deep search capabilities are essential. However, its limitations are in fulfilling optimality and completeness requirements. These aspects must be addressed through modifications or by combining it with other search algorithms. We will dwell upon iterative deepening depth first search (IDDFS).

2.6 Iterative Deepening Depth First Search (IDDFS)

Iterative Deepening Depth-First Search (IDDFS) is a hybrid algorithm that combines the memory efficiency of Depth-First Search (DFS) with the completeness and optimality of Breadth-First Search (BFS). It is particularly useful for problems with large or infinite state spaces where the depth of the solution is unknown.

- Iterative deepening depth first search (aho known as Interactive Deep learning Search) combines the benefits of depth-first search and breadth-first search.
- IDDFS is a general strategy often used in combination with depth-first search; it finds the best depth limit.
- It does this by gradually increasing the limit:
    - First = 0
    - Then = 1
    - Then = 2
    - And so on until a goal is found.
- This will occur where the depth limit reaches "d" the depth of the shallowest goal mode.

2.6.1 IDDFS Algorithm

...(Function ITERATIVE DEEPENING SEARCH (PROBLEM)
Returns a solution as a failure

For depth = O to as do
Result – Depth limited search (problem depth) if result = cut off then return result.

2.3

The iterative deepening search algorithm repeatedly applies **depth-limited search** with increasing limits. It searches **depth-first** but gradually increases the **depth limit**. It states when a solution is formed or if the depth limited search returns failure meaning that no solution units.

2.6.2 Properties of IDDFS Search Algorithms

1. **Completeness**
   - It is **complete** (like BFS) when the branching factor **is finet.**
   - It is also complete for **FINITE GRAPHS** with finet branching as it will eventually reaching mode that is reachable.
2. **Optimality**
   - IDDFS is **optimal**. (Guarantees a **solution** with least path cost) when the path cost is a mandamusing function of the depth.

   For Weighted Graphs IDDES is more optional for weighted graphics unless all edge weight are equal.
3. **Time Complexity**
   - **General Case: The time complexity** of IDDFS is given in equation 2.4

$$O(B^D) \quad \text{.........................2.4}$$

   Where **"b"** is the **branching factor "d"** is the depth of the Shallowest Goal.

   Explanation: Although nodes are visited **multiple times across iterations**, the **overhead** (the amount of time taken to complete the task of reaching the goal at the shallowest level) is **linear** resulting in time complexity similar to BFS.
4. **Space Complexity**
   - Space complexity measures the amount of memory an algorithm uses based on the input size. IDDFS Space Complexity: General case: The space complexity of IDDFS is of the where d is the depth.

Figure 2.6 illustrates the IDDF tree.

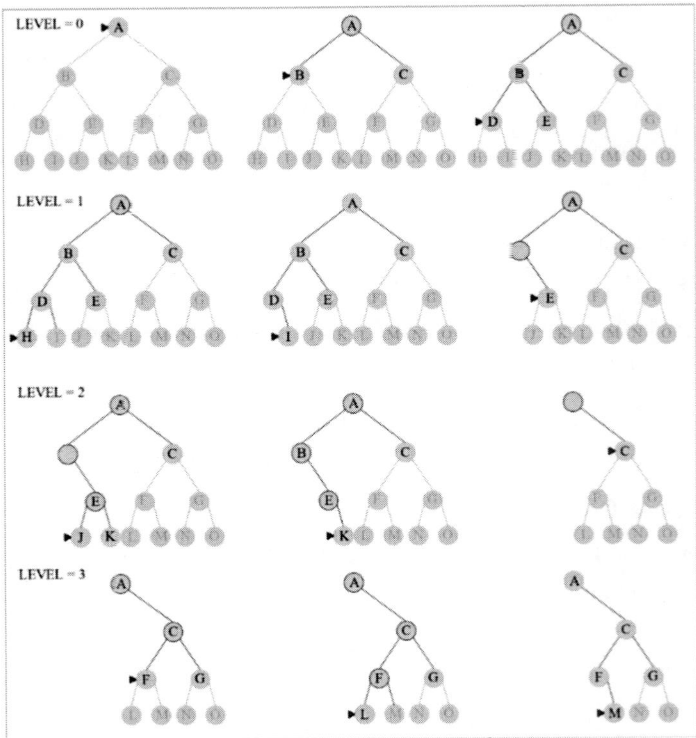

Figure 2.6 Iterative Deepening Depth-First Search (IDDFS)

2.6.3 How IDDFS Works?

IDDFS performs a series of depth-limited searches, incrementally increasing the depth limit until a solution is found. At each iteration, it explores nodes up to the current depth limit using DFS, restarting from the root node for the next deeper limit.

Algorithm Steps

1. **Initialization:**
    - Start at the initial state and set the depth limit to 0.
2. **Depth-Limited Search:**
    - Perform a DFS with the current depth limit.
    - If a solution is found, terminate and return the solution.

- If no solution is found, increase the depth limit and restart the search.

3. **Iteration:**
   - Repeat the process until the solution is found or all possible states are explored.

2.6.4 Examples of IDDFS in AI

1) Path Finding in Mazes, 2) Solving Puzzles 3) Game Tree Exploration: Chess or Crackers, 4) Finding Connected Components, and 5) AI Planning

In the Figure 2.7 **8-puzzle problem** is presented

9	2	8	4
	5	3	7
5	1	4	10
3	14	6	12

Initial State

1	2	3	4
5	6	7	8
9	10	11	12
13	14	15	

Goal state

Figure 2.7 A 4x4 8 Puzzle

Table 2.2 Provides the Comparison of IDDFS with Other Algorithms.

Aspect	IDDFS	DFS	BFS
Completeness	Guaranteed	Not guaranteed in infinite spaces	Guaranteed
Optimality	Guaranteed for uniform-cost problems	Not guaranteed	Guaranteed for uniform-cost problems
Memory Efficiency	O(d)	O(d)	$O(b^d)$
Time Complexity	$O(b^d)$	$O(b^d)$	$O(b^d)$

Example of IDDFS

Consider finding a solution in a simple tree structure:

a) **Depth Limit = 0**: Explore only the root node.

b) **Depth Limit = 1**: Explore all nodes at depth 1 (children of the root).

c) **Depth Limit = 2**: Explore all nodes at depth 2 (grandchildren of the root).

d) Continue this process until the goal node is found.

2.6.5 Advantages of (IDDFS)

1. **Completeness:**
   - IDDFS is complete, ensuring that a solution will be found if one exists, even in infinite state spaces.
2. **Optimality:**
   - Like BFS, IDDFS finds the optimal solution (in terms of the shortest path) in uniform-cost search scenarios.
3. **Memory Efficiency:**
   - IDDFS uses memory proportional to the depth of the current search (O(d)), similar to DFS, making it far more space-efficient than BFS ($O(b^d)$.
4. **Balanced Approach:**
   - Combines the systematic exploration of BFS with the low memory requirements of DFS.

2.6.6 Disadvantages of (IDDFS)

1. **Repeated Exploration:**
   - Nodes near the root are explored multiple times across iterations, leading to redundant computations. However, this overhead is often manageable compared to BFS's memory requirements.

2. **Time Complexity:**
    - Although the asymptotic time complexity is O(bd), the repeated exploration can slightly increase actual runtime compared to BFS.

2.6.7 Applications of IDDFS

1. **Path finding in Graphs:**
    - IDDFS is widely used in large graphs or trees where the solution depth is unknown.
2. **Game Trees:**
    - In game tree exploration, IDDFS helps find solutions in games like chess, where the depth of the solution may vary.
3. **Artificial Intelligence (AI):**
    - Used in AI systems to search through state spaces efficiently with limited memory resources.
4. **Robotics:**
    - IDDFS is employed in navigation systems where both completeness and memory efficiency are critical.

IDDFS is a versatile algorithm that strikes a balance between memory efficiency and solution completeness, making it highly effective for AI and graph-related problems.

Chapter 2: Summary

This chapter focused on the concept of problem-solving in Artificial Intelligence and explained how intelligent agents solve problems using search techniques. It introduced problem-solving agents and described how goals are transformed into well-defined problems by specifying the initial state, possible actions, state transitions, and goal tests. Through example problems, the chapter demonstrated how different real-world tasks can be modeled in a structured form suitable for computational processing.

The chapter also covered the process of searching for solutions and presented important uninformed search strategies, namely Breadth-First Search, Depth-First Search, and Iterative Deepening Depth-First Search. Each strategy was explained in terms of how it explores the problem space and the advantages and limitations associated with time, space, and completeness. These methods provide the basic framework for understanding systematic exploration in AI problem-solving.

Problem-solving through search is a fundamental capability of intelligent agents in Artificial Intelligence. The concepts discussed in this chapter form the basis for understanding how agents reason, plan, and make decisions to achieve goals in different environments. Although uninformed search strategies do not use additional knowledge about the problem domain, they play a crucial role in establishing core search principles.

By studying problem-solving agents and uninformed search techniques, learners gain essential insights into the strengths and weaknesses of different approaches to search. This knowledge serves as a strong foundation for advanced topics such as heuristic and informed search strategies, which build upon the ideas introduced in this chapter.

Conclusion

Problem-solving and search form the core of intelligent behavior in Artificial Intelligence. This chapter established how agents convert goals into structured problems and systematically explore possible solutions using uninformed search strategies. By understanding Breadth-First Search, Depth-First Search, and Iterative Deepening Depth-First Search, learners recognize the trade-offs between time, space, completeness, and efficiency in different search approaches.

Although uninformed methods operate without domain-specific knowledge, they provide the essential theoretical and practical foundation for all subsequent search and reasoning techniques. Mastery of these basic strategies enables students to appreciate how intelligent agents plan actions, evaluate alternatives, and progress toward goals. The principles learned here serve as a stepping stone to more advanced informed and heuristic search methods, strengthening the overall understanding of AI problem-solving mechanisms.

Chapter – 3

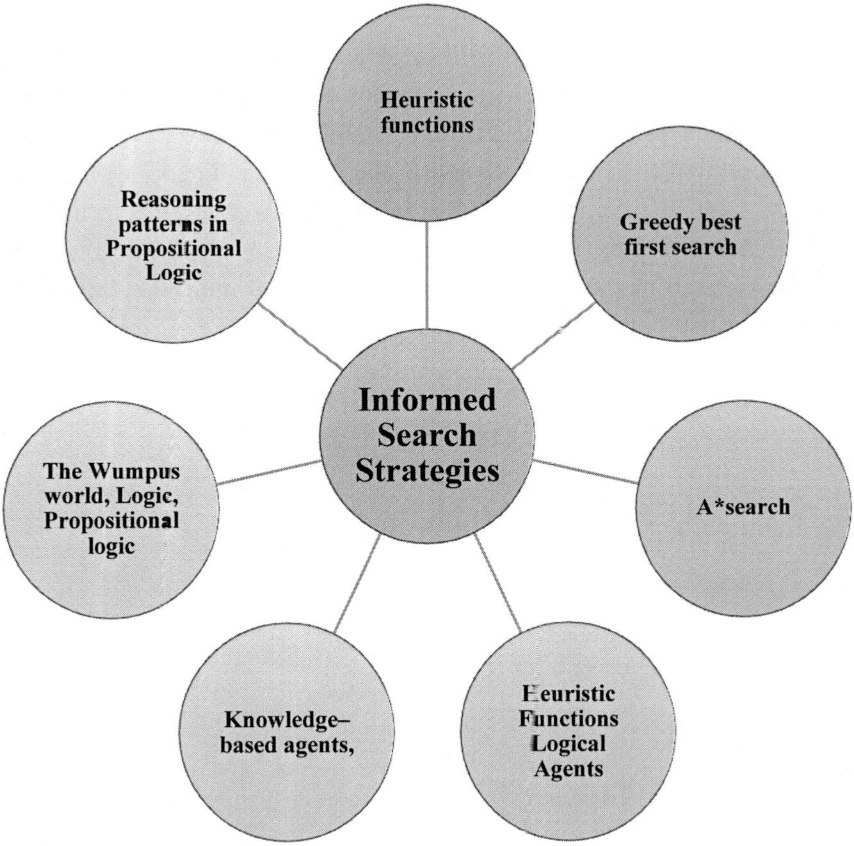
Heuristic functions
Greedy best first search
A*search
Heuristic Functions Logical Agents
Knowledge–based agents,
The Wumpus world, Logic, Propositional logic
Reasoning patterns in Propositional Logic
Informed Search Strategies

3.0 Introduction to Informed Search Strategies

Many real-world issues in artificial intelligence. can be described as search problems, where an intelligent agent must decide on a series of actions to move from an initial state into a desired goal state. The search approach employed has a major impact on how well such problems are solved. In general, there are two types of search methods: **informed (heuristic)** search strategies and **uninformed (blind)** search strategies.

To more effectively steer the search process toward the objective, informed search strategies leverage extra problem-specific knowledge. Unlike uninformed search methods, which explore the search space without any guidance, informed search strategies use an evaluation function to estimate how promising a particular state is.

This significantly decreases the number of visited states by enabling the algorithm to expand the most relevant nodes first. Utilizing heuristic information—knowledge gained from experience, domain knowledge, or approximation techniques—to enhance decision-making during search is the fundamental concept behind informed search. Informed search strategies frequently yield faster results with lower computing costs in terms of time and memory by giving priority to nodes that appear closer to the goal.

In large or complex state spaces, where complete investigation is impractical, informed search tactics are particularly crucial. Path finding, gaming, robotics, scheduling, planning, and optimization issues are just a few of the fields in which they are frequently used. Greedy Best-First Search, A* search, and hill climbing are examples of common informed search algorithms that use heuristic functions to direct their operations.

3.1 Heuristic Functions

An essential part of well-informed strategies for searching is a heuristic function. It provides an estimate of the cost or distance it will take to get from one state to the goal state. The notation for heuristic functions is h(n), where n is a node in the search tree and h(n) is an estimate of the node's proximity to the goal.

Heuristics are created with domain knowledge and are problem-specific. Heuristics, in contrast to exact algorithms, do not promise perfect accuracy; rather, their objective is to produce accurate approximations that aid the search algorithm in making better choices. By minimizing unnecessary investigation, a well-designed heuristic can significantly increase a search's efficiency.

3.1.1 Role of Heuristic Functions

The primary role of a heuristic function is to **guide the search process** by ranking nodes according to their estimated desirability. Nodes with lower heuristic values are typically considered closer to the goal and are expanded first. This prioritization allows informed search algorithms to focus on promising paths rather than exploring the entire search space.

Characteristics of Good Heuristics

A heuristic function should ideally have the following properties:

- **Admissibility**: It never overestimates the true cost to reach the goal.
- **Consistency (Monotonicity)**: The heuristic estimate is always less than or equal to the cost of reaching a neighbouring node plus the heuristic of that neighbour.
- **Efficiency**: It should be computationally inexpensive to evaluate.
- **Accuracy**: It should provide estimates that are as close as possible to the actual cost.

Examples of Heuristic Functions

- In **route-finding problems**, straight-line distance to the destination is commonly used as a heuristic.
- In the **8-puzzle problem**, heuristics such as the **number of misplaced tiles** or **Manhattan distance** are widely applied.
- In **game playing**, heuristics evaluate board positions based on factors like material advantage or positional strength.

3.1.2 Importance in Informed Search

Heuristic functions transform uninformed search into informed search by embedding **intelligence. and experience** into the algorithm. The effectiveness of an informed search strategy largely depends on the quality of its heuristic function. Poor heuristics may lead to inefficient searches, while strong heuristics can yield near-optimal performance.

In summary, heuristic functions serve as the **guiding intelligence**. of informed search strategies, enabling AI systems to solve complex problems efficiently and realistically.

3.2 Greedy Best-First Search (GBFS)

Greedy Best-First Search is that prioritizes exploration of nodes based on a heuristic function. Unlike uninformed search algorithms, GBFS uses domain-specific knowledge to make decisions, aiming to move toward the goal state as quickly as possible.

The Figure 3.1 illustrates how Greedy Best-First Search selects and expands the node with the lowest heuristic value h(n), moving toward the goal based only on estimated closeness.

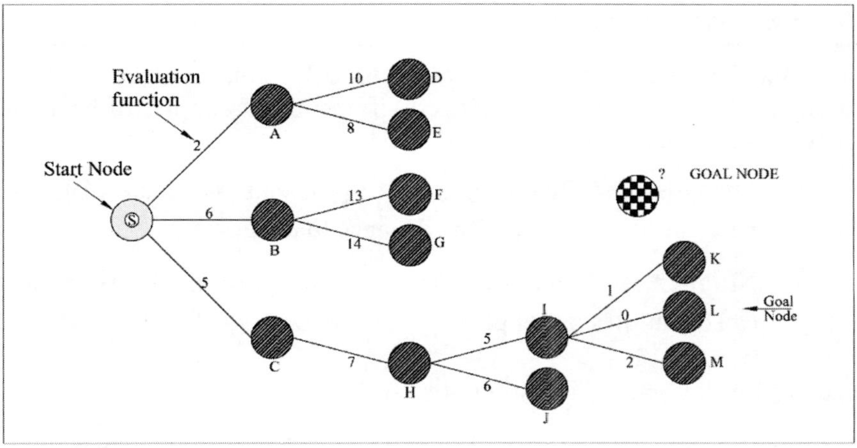

Figure 3.1 Greedy Best First Search Graph

3.2.1 How Greedy Best-First Search Works?

GBFS evaluates nodes using a heuristic function h(n), which estimates the cost to reach the goal from the current node n. It selects the node with the lowest h(n) value for expansion, operating under the assumption that this node is closest to the goal.

3.2.2 Algorithm Steps

1. **Initialization:**
   - Place the initial node in a priority queue.

- Priority is based on the heuristic value h(n).

2. **Exploration:**
   - Remove the node with the smallest h(n) from the queue.
   - If it is the goal state, terminate and return the solution.
   - If not, expand the node and add its neighbours to the queue, evaluating their heuristic values.
3. **Iteration:**
4. **Repeat the process until the queue is empty or the goal is reached.**

3.2.3 Heuristic Function

The **heuristic function h(n)** is central to GBFS and must be carefully designed for the algorithm to perform efficiently. Examples of heuristic functions include:

- **Straight-Line Distance**: Used in problems like route planning, where h(n) is the Euclidean distance to the goal.
- **Number of Misplaced Tiles**: In puzzles like the 8 Puzzle, h(n) can count tiles out of place compared to the goal state.

Example: Navigating a Graph with GBFS

Consider a graph representing cities, where the goal is to find the shortest route to a target city. GBFS evaluates cities based on their straight-line distance to the target and chooses the one closest to the goal for exploration.

3.2.4 Advantages of (GBFS)

1. **Efficiency:**
   - GBFS is faster than uninformed search algorithms like Breadth-First Search (BFS) because it uses a heuristic to focus on promising paths.
2. **Focus on Goal:**
   - It prioritizes exploration toward the goal, reducing the number of nodes visited in many cases.

3. **Simple to Implement:**
    - The use of a priority queue makes GBFS relatively straightforward to code.

3.2.5 Disadvantages of (GBFS)

1. **Non-Optimal:**
    - GBFS does not guarantee finding the shortest or least-cost solution. It may choose suboptimal paths due to reliance solely on h(n).
2. **Incomplete:**
    - If the heuristic leads to a dead-end or an infinite loop, GBFS may fail to find a solution unless additional mechanisms (e.g., cycle detection) are used.
3. **Heuristic Dependence:**
    - The performance of GBFS is highly dependent on the quality of the heuristic function. Poor heuristics can make the algorithm inefficient or incorrect.

3.2.6 Applications of (GBFS)

1. **Path finding:**
    - Used in navigation systems where speed is more critical than optimality.
2. **Game Playing:**
    - Applied in decision-making for games like chess or puzzles to prioritize promising moves.
3. **Robotics.:**
    - GBFS helps robots plan paths to target locations efficiently.

GBFS is a valuable algorithm in Artificial Intelligence (AI), offering a fast, heuristic-driven approach to problem-solving. However, its lack of optimality and completeness nice.

3.3 A* Search Algorithm

The A* search algorithm combines the benefits of Breadth-First Search (BFS) with Depth-First Search (DFS), rendering it a well-known and informed search strategy. It employs a heuristic method to efficiently explore the state space while ensuring the shortest path to the goal, assuming the heuristic is admissible (does not overestimate the cost).

3.3.1 How A* Search Works?

A* uses an evaluation function f(n) to determine the priority of nodes for exploration. The evaluation function is defined as:

$$f(n)=g(n) + h(n) \quad \text{.....................3.1}$$

The Figure 3.2 shows that the A* algorithm uses the evaluation function f(n)=g(n)+h(n), which combines the actual path cost g(n) and the heuristic estimate h(n) to select the most optimal node for expansion.

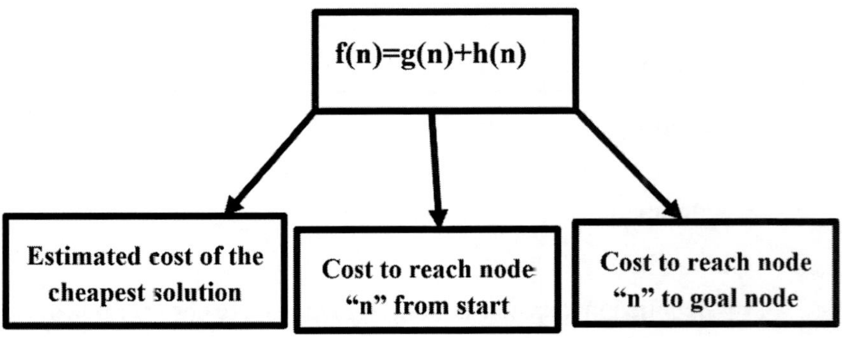

Figure 3.2 Evaluation Function f(n) in A* Algorithm

Where:

- **g**(n): The cost of the path from the start node to the current node n.
- **h**(n): A heuristic estimate of the cost from n to the goal node.

The algorithm selects nodes with the lowest (n), ensuring a balance between the actual and anticipated costs to reach the goal.

3.3.2 A* Algorithm Steps

1. **Initialization:**
   - Create a priority queue (open list) and add the start node with its f(n) value.
   - Maintain a closed list to track explored nodes.
2. **Node Expansion:**
   - Dequeue the node with the lowest f(n) from the open list.
   - If the node is the goal, terminate and reconstruct the path.
3. **Successor Generation:**
   - Generate all successors of the current node.
   - Calculate g(n), h(n), and f(n) for each successor.
4. **Update Open List:**
   - If a successor is not in the open or closed list, add it to the open list.
   - If a successor is already in the open list with a higher f(n), update it with the lower value.
5. **Repeat:**
   - Continue until the goal is reached or the open list is empty (indicating no solution exists).

3.3.3 Key Properties of A*

1. **Admissibility:**
   - A* is admissible if the heuristic h(n) is non-overestimating, ensuring it finds an optimal solution.
2. **Consistency (Monotonicity):**
   - A consistent heuristic satisfies $h(n) \leq c(n,n') + h(n')$, where $c(n,n')$ is the cost of transitioning between nodes n and n’

Consistency guarantees that f(n) values are non-decreasing along a path.

3. **Optimality:**
   - A* guarantees an optimal solution if the heuristic is admissible and consistent.

3.3.4 Advantages of A*

1. **Efficiency:**
   - A* intelligently explores the most promising paths first, reducing unnecessary exploration.
2. **Guaranteed Optimality:**
   - Finds the shortest path to the goal if the heuristic is admissible.
3. **Flexible Heuristics:**
   - Heuristics can be tailored to specific problems for improved performance.

3.3.5 Disadvantages of A*

1. **Memory Intensive:**
   - A* stores all explored and frontier nodes, which can lead to high memory usage for large problems.
2. **Heuristic Sensitivity:**
   - The efficiency of A* heavily depends on the quality of the heuristic function. Poor heuristics can result in suboptimal performance.

3.3.6 Applications of A*

1. **Path finding:**
   - Widely used in games and robotics for finding optimal paths.
   - **Example**: Navigating through a maze or map.
2. **Puzzle Solving:**
   - Used for solving problems like the 8 Puzzle and 15 Puzzle.

3. **Route Planning:**
    - Applied in GPS systems for determining the shortest or fastest route between locations.

Table 3.1 Comparison of GBFS with A* algorithm

Aspect	Greedy Best-First Search	*A Search Algorithm**
Evaluation Function	h(n) (heuristic estimate to goal)	f(algn)=g(n)+h(n) (cost so far + heuristic estimate)
Optimality	Not guaranteed	Guaranteed if h(n) is admissible
Completeness	Not guaranteed	Guaranteed if a solution exists
Focus	Focuses entirely on heuristic	Balances heuristic with path cost

3.4 Logical Agents and Knowledge-Based Agents

We, the Humans possess knowledge, and this knowledge enables US to act intelligently in the world. Human intelligence. is not governed merely by reflex actions, but by the ability to **reason using internally represented knowledge**. Artificial Intelligence adopts this same principle through **logical agents**, which represent information about the world in a formal language and use reasoning processes to decide what actions to take. Thus, logical agents embody the idea that intelligence arises from **thinking with knowledge**, rather than reacting blindly to stimuli. In other words, *thus, logical agents embody the idea that intelligence arises from thinking with knowledge, rather than reacting blindly to* **sensor inputs and directly triggering effector actions**.

This view of intelligence. is realized in AI systems as **knowledge-based agents**, which are practical implementations of logical agents. In such agents, knowledge about the world is explicitly stored in a **knowledge base**, and logical inference is used to derive new conclusions and select appropriate actions. By continuously updating their knowledge from percepts and reasoning about the consequences of actions, knowledge-based agents can behave rationally in complex environments. Hence, logical agents provide the **theoretical foundation**, while knowledge-based agents represent the **architectural embodiment** of reasoning-based intelligence.

3.4.1 Knowledge-Based Agents

Knowledge-based agents are a type of intelligent agent that leverages stored knowledge to make informed decisions and solve problems. These agents rely on a **knowledge base (KB)**, which is a structured repository of facts, rules, and information about their environment. The knowledge base is used in conjunction with an inference engine to derive new information and make decisions. Intelligent agents require knowledge about the real world to make decisions and reason efficiently. **Knowledge-based agents** are a specialized type of intelligent agents with the ability to:

- Maintain an internal state of knowledge.
- Reason over that knowledge to draw conclusions.
- Update their knowledge base based on observations.
- Take informed actions accordingly.

These agents use a **formal representation** of the world to reason and act intelligently. They are composed of two primary components:

1. **Knowledge Base (KB):**
   - A structured repository of facts, rules, and information about the world.
   - Enables the agent to store and retrieve knowledge for reasoning.
2. **Inference. System:**
   - A mechanism to apply logical reasoning to the knowledge base.
   - Allows the agent to deduce new facts, resolve uncertainties, and identify appropriate actions.

3.4.2 Capabilities of a Knowledge-Based Agent.

A knowledge-based agent must possess the following capabilities:

- **Representation**: It should represent states, actions, and other world elements using a formal language.

- **Incorporation of New Precepts**: It should update its knowledge base dynamically with new information from the environment.
- **Internal Representation Updates**: It should refine its internal model of the world as new observations are made.
- **Reasoning**: It should deduce facts and infer the state of the world based on available knowledge.
- **Action Deduction**: It should determine and execution appropriate actions based on its reasoning process.

This combination of knowledge representation, reasoning, and decision-making allows knowledge-based agents to act intelligently and adapt to complex environments.

3.4.3 Key features of knowledge-based agents include

1. **Knowledge Representation:**
   - The agent uses formal languages (e.g., propositional or first-order logic) to represent facts and rules.
   - This allows for reasoning about the environment in a structured and interpretable way.
2. **Decision-Making:**
   - Based on the stored knowledge, the agent evaluates possible actions and selects the one that aligns with its goals.
   - The reasoning process involves applying inference techniques to deduce new facts or resolve uncertainties.
3. **Dynamic Updates:**
   - The agent continuously updates its knowledge base as it perceives new information from the environment.
   - This makes the agent adaptable and capable of handling dynamic scenarios.

The Figure 3.3 shows the Knowledge-Based Agent architecture, where the agent uses a knowledge base and inference mechanism to perceive information, reason about it, and take appropriate actions.

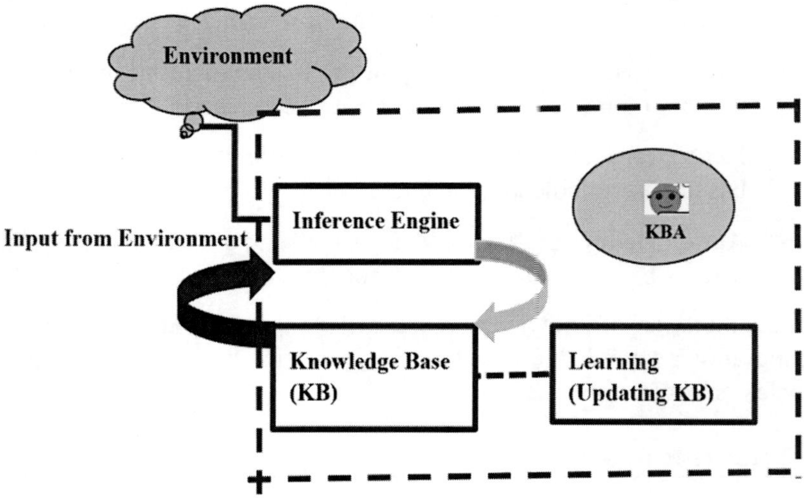

Figure 3.3 The Knowledge-Based Agent. Architecture

3.4.4 Operations Performed by (KBA)

Following are three operations which are performed by KBA in order to show the intelligent behaviour:

a) **TELL:** This operation tells the knowledge base what it perceives from the environment.

b) **ASK:** This operation asks the knowledge base what action it should perform.

c) **Perform:** It performs the selected action.

Knowledge Base (KB)

The **knowledge base** is a central component of a knowledge-based agent (KBA)} and is often referred to as KB. It is a collection of **sentences *(a technical term distinct from sentences in natural language)*** that represent facts about the world. These sentences are expressed in a structured **knowledge representation language** Knowledge Representation Language, enabling the agent to store and manipulate knowledge systematically.

Why Use a Knowledge Base?

A knowledge base is essential for:

- **Updating Knowledge**: It allows the agent to incorporate new information from its environment.
- **Learning from Experience**: The KB evolves as the agent interacts with the world.
- **Informed Decision-Making**: Actions are guided by the accumulated and processed knowledge in the KB.

Inference. System

The **inference system** is responsible for deriving new sentences from existing ones in the knowledge base (KB). This process, known as **inference**, enables the agent to expand its understanding and take appropriate actions. A sentence, in this context, is a proposition or assertion about the world.

The inference system applies **logical rules** to the KB, deducing new information that the agent can use to update its knowledge base and reason about the world effectively.

Working of the Inference. System

The inference system operates using two primary methods:

1. **Forward Chaining**
    - Starts with known facts in the KB and applies inference rules to deduce new facts.
    - Useful for deriving all possible conclusions from given knowledge.
2. **Backward Chaining**
    - Begins with a goal or query and works backward to determine if the goal can be satisfied using the knowledge in the KB.
    - Efficient for answering specific questions or achieving targeted objectives.

By integrating the **knowledge base** and **inference system**, a knowledge-based agent can effectively reason, learn, and act in dynamic environments, ensuring intelligent behaviour.

3.4.5 Examples of Knowledge-Based Agents (KBA)

1. **Medical Diagnosis System**
   - **Use Case**: A system used by healthcare professionals to diagnose diseases.
   - **Knowledge Base**: Contains medical facts, symptoms, diseases, and their relationships (e.g., "Fever and rash suggest measles").
   - **Inference. System**: Uses forward chaining to analyze symptoms and deduce potential diseases, or backward chaining to verify a suspected diagnosis.
   - **Example in Action**: A patient reports fever and fatigue. The system infers possible conditions like flu or dengue, and suggests tests for confirmation.
2. **Virtual Personal Assistants**
3. **Use Case:** Virtual assistants like Siri, Alexa, or Google Assistant.
4. **Knowledge Base:** Stores information about user preferences, tasks, weather, and events.
   - **Inference. System**: Infers appropriate actions, such as setting a reminder when you say, “Remind me to call John tomorrow at 10 AM.”
   - **Example in Action**: If the user asks, “Do I have any meetings today?” the system checks the knowledge base (calendar entries) and responds accordingly.

3.5 The Wumpus World

The **Wumpus World** is a classic problem in artificial intelligence. used to illustrate reasoning under uncertainty., the design of knowledge-based agents, and the use of logical inference. It is a grid-based environment where an agent navigates a world filled with hazards, aiming to achieve its goal while avoiding dangers.

3.5.1 Components of the Wumpus World

1. **Grid Environment:**
   - The world is a square grid (e.g., 4x4), and each cell can contain objects or hazards.

2. **Objects and Hazards:**
   - **Agent.:** The player-controlled entity that explores the grid.
   - **Gold:** The goal of the game; the agent must locate and retrieve the gold.
   - **Pits:** Deadly holes falling into a pit results in the agent's death.
   - **Wumpus:** A dangerous monster that kills the agent if entered into its cell.
3. **Precepts:**
   - **Breeze:** Felt in a cell adjacent to a pit.
   - **Bump:** Experienced when the agent tries to move into a wall.
   - **Glitter:** Observed in a cell containing gold

The Figure 3.4 represents a 4×4 grid Wumpus World environment where an agent navigates to find gold while avoiding dangers like pits and the Wumpus using percepts and logical reasoning.

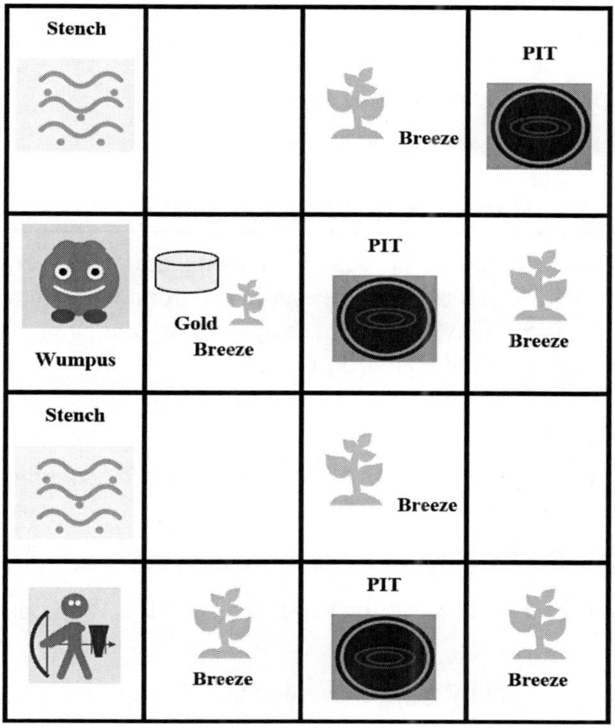

Figure 3.4 The Wumpus World (4x4 grid)

- **Scream:** Heard when the Wumpus is killed by the agent.
- **Stench:** Detected in a cell adjacent to the Wumpus.

3.5.2 Goal of the Agent

The agent's objective is to locate and retrieve the gold while avoiding pits and the Wumpus. After finding the gold, the agent must return safely to its starting position.

1. **Agent. Actions:**
    - Move forward
    - Turn left or right
    - Grab the gold
    - Shoot an arrow (to potentially kill the Wumpus)
2. **Strategy Considerations:**
    - The agent must use logical reasoning and probabilistic inference
    - Must map the world with limited sensory information
    - Needs to avoid deadly squares
    - Balance exploration with safety

3.5.3 PEAS Description of the Wumpus World

The **Wumpus World** can be described using the **PEAS framework**, which defines the Performance measure, Environment, Actuators, and Sensors of an agent. This framework helps outline the agent's objectives and its interactions with the environment.

Performance Measure

The agent's success in the Wumpus World is evaluated using the following performance measures:

- **+1000 Points**: Reward for safely exiting the cave with the gold.
- **-1000 Points**: Penalty for being eaten by the Wumpus or falling into a pit.
- **-1 Point**: Penalty for each action taken (e.g., moving, turning).
- **-10 Points**: Penalty for using an arrow to attempt killing the Wumpus.

The Game Ends When Either

- The agent successfully escapes with the gold.
- The agent dies by encountering the Wumpus or falling into a pit.

This performance measure incentivizes efficient, cautious exploration and prioritizes the agent's survival and task completion.

Implementation Techniques

- Often solved using:
- Propositional logic
- First-order logic
- Probabilistic reasoning algorithms
- Search algorithms like A*

3.5.4 Reasoning in the Wumpus World

The Wumpus World requires the agent to use logical reasoning to deduce the safest and most efficient path. The agent must update its **knowledge base** based on its **precepts** and make decisions using the **inference system**

Forward Chaining:

Starts with known facts (e.g., "Breeze is felt in this cell") and infers the possible locations of pits.

Backward Chaining:

Starts with a goal (e.g., "Is it safe to move to cell [2,2]?") and works backward using rules to verify safety.

Example Scenario

a) The agent starts in a corner of the grid.

b) It perceives a **breeze**, indicating one or more pits in adjacent cells.

c) Using logical inference, the agent deduces the possible locations of pits and marks them as dangerous.

d) It perceives a **stench** near another cell, inferring the Wumpus's possible location.

e) It avoids dangerous cells, locates the **gold**, and safely returns to the starting point.

The **Wumpus World** is a powerful tool for teaching knowledge-based reasoning, decision-making, and the integration of perceptual data into an agent's behaviour. It demonstrates how agents use a combination of their **knowledge base**, **precepts**, and **logical inference** to act intelligently in uncertain environments.

3.6 Logic, Propositional Logic, Reasoning Patterns in Propositional Logic

Logic is the study of reasoning and formal systems of thought. In artificial intelligence. (AI), logic provides a foundational framework for representing knowledge, reasoning, and enabling intelligent agents to make decisions. Logic allows agents to process facts, deduce new information, and take actions in a structured and interpretable way. Logic in AI focuses on creating systems that can emulate human reasoning. It is used to formalize how AI agents represent knowledge about their environment and reason about it. Logic ensures that an AI agent's decisions are consistent, rational, and explainable.

3.6.1 Types of Logic in AI

1. **Propositional Logic:**
    - Deals with propositions (statements) and their relationships using logical connectives.
    - **Example**: "If the sky is clear, then it is not raining."
2. **First-Order Logic (FOL):**
    - Extends propositional logic by including quantifiers and relations between objects.
    - **Example**: "For all people, if someone is a student, they attend classes."
3. **Modal Logic:**
4. **Represents possibilities, necessities, or beliefs.**
    - **Example**: "It is possible that the agent will win the game."
5. **Temporal Logic:**
    - Focuses on reasoning about time-based events.
    - **Example**: "If the alarm rings, the agent will leave the building within 5 minutes."

6. **Fuzzy Logic:**
   - Handles reasoning under uncertainty. with degrees of truth rather than binary true/false values.
   - **Example**: "The weather is somewhat sunny today", "The weather is moderately warm."

3.6.2 Reasoning in AI: Deductive, Inductive, and Abductive Logics

AI agents employ different types of reasoning, depending on the problem context and the nature of available information.

1. **Deductive Reasoning:**
   - Derives logically certain conclusions from general rules and specific facts.
   - **Example in AI:**
     - ❖ **Rule**: "All humans are mortal."
     - ❖ **Fact**: "Socrates is a human."
     - ❖ **Conclusion**: "Socrates is mortal."
   - Deductive reasoning is common in knowledge-based systems where certainty is required.
2. **Inductive Reasoning:**
   - Generalizes patterns or rules from specific observations.
   - **Example in AI:**
     - ❖ **Observations**: "The sun rose today, yesterday, and the day before."
     - ❖ **Conclusion**: "The sun rises every day."
   - Inductive reasoning is used in machine learning to identify patterns in data.
3. **Abductive Reasoning:**
   - Infers the most plausible explanation for an observation.
   - **Example in AI:**
     - ❖ **Observation**: "The ground is wet."
     - ❖ **Hypothesis**: "It rained."
     - ❖ Abductive reasoning is common in diagnostic systems and hypothesis generation.

3.6.3 Propositional Logic

Propositional Logic is a formal system used for reasoning about propositions (statements) and their relationships. In artificial intelligence. (AI), propositional logic provides a foundation for creating rules and reasoning systems, enabling AI agents to make decisions and draw conclusions based on facts.

The Figure 3.5 illustrates the main logical connectives in propositional logic—such as AND, OR, NOT, implication, and biconditional—and how they combine propositions to form logical expressions.

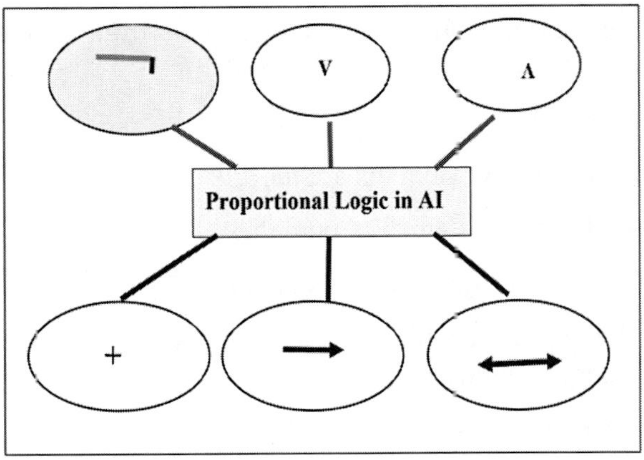

Figure 3.5 Logical Connectives of Propositional Logic

Propositions: A **proposition** is a declarative statement that can be either **true** or **false**, but not both.

Example:

- **p**: "The light is on."
- **q**: "The room is empty."

Propositional Variables

- Propositional logic uses variables. (e.g., p,q,r,s) to represent propositions.
- Each variable can hold a truth value:
- **True** (T) or
- **False** (F).

Propositional Connectives

Propositional connectives are symbols used to combine or modify propositions to express logical relationships. These connectives are fundamental in programming AI agents to evaluate and act based on logical conditions.

Common Propositional Connectives:

7. **Negation (¬)**
   - **a)** Represents "NOT."
   - **b)** If p is true, ¬p (not p) is false, and vice versa.
   - **c)** **Example**: If p = "It is raining," ¬p= "It is not raining."

8. **Conjunction (∧)**
   1. Represents "AND."
   2. True only when both propositions are true.
   3. **Example**: p∧q = "The light is on AND the room is empty."

9. **Disjunction (∨)**
   1. Represents "OR."
   2. True if at least one of the propositions is true.
   3. **Example**: p∨q = "The light is on OR the room is empty."

10. **Implication (→)**
    1. Represents "IF..THEN."
    2. **p→q**: If p is true, then q must be true. If p is false, the implication is always true.
    3. **Example**: "If it is raining (p), then the ground is wet (q)."

11. **Biconditional (↔) Biconditional (↔}**
    1. Represents "IF AND ONLY IF."
    2. True when both propositions are either true or false.
    3. **Example**: p↔q = "The light is on IF AND ONLY IF the room is empty."

Propositional Logic in AI Agents

Propositional logic is used in AI agents to encode rules and reason about the world.

How It Works?

1. **Representation of Rules:**
    1. Rules are encoded using propositional logic.
    2. **Example**: "If there is a stench (p), then there is a Wumpus nearby (q)" is written as p→q.
2. **Inference.:**
    1. AI agents use inference systems (e.g., forward chaining or backward chaining) to derive conclusions from a knowledge base.
    2. **Example**: If p (stench is detected), infer q (Wumpus is nearby).
3. **Decision-Making:**
    1. Logical connectives help agents evaluate multiple conditions.
    2. **Example: "Move to a cell only if it is safe (¬p∧¬q)"**

Summary of Key Points

- **Propositions:** Statements that are either true or false.
- **Connectives:** Combine propositions to represent complex rules and conditions.
    - **¬: Negation (NOT).**
    - **∧: Conjunction (AND).**
    - **∨: Disjunction (OR).**
    - **→: Implication (IF..THEN).**
    - **↔: Biconditional (IF AND ONLY IF).**

Usage in AI

- Represent knowledge about the environment.
- Enable logical inference for decision-making.
- Program rules for AI agents to reason effectively.

This logical framework enables AI systems to analyse, reason, and act based on a structured representation of the world.

3.6.4 Reasoning Patterns in Propositional Logic

Reasoning patterns in propositional logic describe the **standard forms of logical inference** used to derive valid conclusions from given premises. These patterns specify how new propositions can be inferred while preserving truth, provided the original statements are true. In artificial intelligence., such reasoning patterns enable logical agents to **deduce implicit knowledge**, verify conclusions, and support rational decision-making within a knowledge base.

Common reasoning patterns include **Modus Ponens**, **Modus Tollens**, **And-Introduction**, **And-Elimination**, **Or-Introduction**, and **Resolution**. These inference rules form the basis of automated reasoning systems and are widely used in knowledge-based agents to answer queries and select actions. By systematically applying these reasoning patterns, AI systems ensure that conclusions are **logically sound, consistent, and explainable**, making propositional logic a fundamental tool for reasoning in intelligent agents.

Chapter 3: Summary

This chapter introduced two major pillars of Artificial Intelligence: **informed search strategies** and **logical reasoning using knowledge-based agents**. Informed search strategies improve problem-solving efficiency by using **heuristic functions** that estimate the closeness of a state to the goal. By incorporating domain knowledge, these strategies guide the search process more intelligently than uninformed methods. Algorithms such as **Greedy Best-First Search** use heuristic values to prioritize node expansion, enabling faster solutions in large and complex search spaces.

The chapter then explored **logical agents**, emphasizing the role of **knowledge representation and reasoning** in intelligent behaviour. Knowledge-based agents store information about the world in a structured form and use logical inference to decide actions. The **Wumpus World** was presented as a classic example to illustrate how agents use percepts, logic, and inference to act rationally in partially observable environments.

Further, the chapter discussed the fundamentals of **logic and propositional logic**, introducing how facts and relationships can be represented using propositional symbols and logical connectives. Finally, various **reasoning patterns in propositional logic** were explained, demonstrating how valid conclusions can be derived from known premises. Together, these topics show how intelligent agents combine **heuristic search** with **logical reasoning** to solve problems effectively.

Conclusions

In conclusion, Chapter 3 highlights that intelligence. in AI systems arises from the **integration of informed problem-solving and logical reasoning**. Heuristic-guided search enables agents to efficiently navigate large state spaces, while knowledge-based reasoning allows them to make consistent and explainable decisions. Informed search strategies reduce computational effort, and logical agents provide a structured approach to understanding and acting within an environment.

By studying heuristic functions, greedy best-first search, and propositional logic, students gain insight into how AI systems move beyond simple reflex behaviour toward **rational, goal-directed action**. The concepts discussed in this chapter form a foundation for advanced topics such as **automated planning, constraint satisfaction, and intelligent decision-making**, reinforcing the importance of combining search and reasoning in the design of intelligent agents.

Chapter – 4

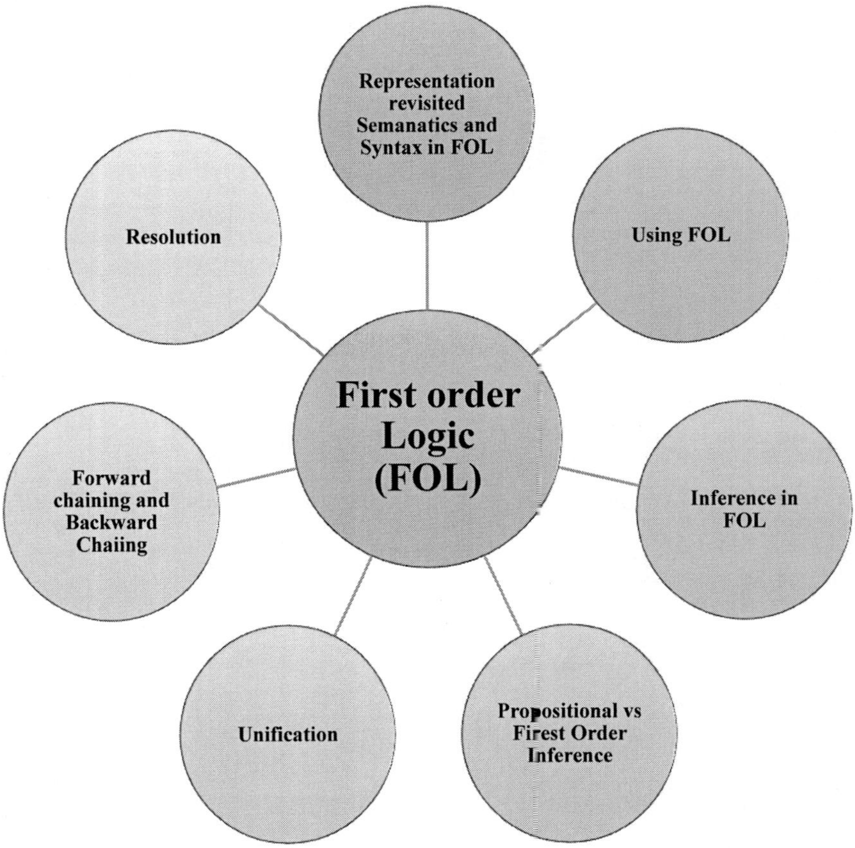
Representation revisited Semanatics and Syntax in FOL
Using FOL
Inference in FOL
Propositional vs Firest Order Inference
Unification
Forward chaining and Backward Chaiing
Resolution
First order Logic (FOL)

Introduction

Artificial Intelligence systems must represent knowledge about complex environments and reason about it in a precise and systematic manner. While propositional logic provides a foundation for logical reasoning, its expressiveness is limited when dealing with real-world domains involving objects, properties, and relationships. To overcome these limitations, **First Order Logic (FOL)** extends propositional logic by introducing variables, quantifiers, predicates, and functions, enabling richer and more flexible knowledge representation. This chapter introduces FOL as a powerful formalism for representing structured knowledge and supporting intelligent reasoning.

This chapter begins by revisiting knowledge representation through the lens of First Order Logic, emphasizing how it models the world or environment as a domain of objects and relations. The chapter then explains the **syntax and semantics of FOL**, clarifying how well-formed logical expressions are constructed and how their meanings are interpreted with respect to a domain of discourse. Understanding both syntax and semantics is essential for ensuring that logical statements are not only correctly formed but also meaningful within the modelled environment.

The chapter further explores **reasoning and inference in First Order Logic**, highlighting how knowledge can be derived from existing facts and rules. Key inference mechanisms such as **unification, forward chaining, backward chaining, and resolution** are discussed, along with a comparison between propositional and first-order inference. These techniques form the basis of logical reasoning in AI systems such as expert systems, knowledge-based agents, and automated theorem provers.

4.0 First Order Logic: Representation Revisited, Syntax and Semantics

By addressing the limitations of propositional logic and providing a more expressive and structured description of the world/environment, First Order Logic (FOL) revisits knowledge representation. Instead of being expressed as discrete facts, knowledge in FOL is expressed in terms of objects, their characteristics, and the connections between them. Through the use of variables and quantifiers, this richer representation enables abstractions and generalizations, enabling the concise statement of existential claims and universal laws. Consequently, FOL allows reasoning about categories, actions, and interactions among entities, making it a potent formalism for modelling real-world domains in AI.

The formal symbols and rules required to create valid expressions are provided in the **syntax** of First Order Logic. Constants, variables, predicate symbols, and function symbols are its core building blocks; these components form together to produce terms and atomic formulas. Formulas are connected/joined by logical connectives like **¬, ∧, ∨, →,** and ↔, and variables are bound/bind and the range of generality is defined by quantifiers like existential **(∃)** and universal **(∀)**. Every well-formed formula is made certain to be precise and clear/unambiguous by the syntactic structure, which also offers a common language for expressing knowledge that automated reasoning systems can understand.

The **semantics** of First Order Logic define the meaning of syntactically correct expressions by interpreting them over a domain of discourse. An interpretation assigns meanings to constants, functions, and predicates, and determines the truth value of formulas under a given model. Semantics bridges the gap between symbolic representation and the real or abstract world being modeled, ensuring that logical statements correspond to intended facts and relationships. Together, syntax and semantics make FOL a robust framework for knowledge representation and reasoning, enabling AI systems to draw valid inferences, verify consistency, and support intelligent decision-making. Bayes

4.1 First-Order Logic (FOL)/First-Order Predicate Logic

First Order Logic (FOL) is a fundamental theoretical framework that has widespread use in fields such as mathematics, philosophy, computer science, and linguistics. It provides a useful framework for expressing and reasoning about the relationships between items in a given domain. FOL broadens/expands propositional logic by including objects, connections, and quantifiers. FOL is more expressive than propositional logic, enabling for the structured representation of complicated/complex facts and reasoning. It is frequently employed in AI for knowledge representation, reasoning, and intelligent system design.

In the discipline of artificial intelligence. (AI), **First-Order Logic (FOL)**, is a foundation/ corner stone for knowledge representation and reasoning. FOL's well-defined syntax and semantics enable the precise storing of information and relationships, making it a reliable/trustworthy tool for AI systems. For example, FOL is utilized in automated reasoning planning and natural language understanding, where its expressiveness permits complex problem-solving and decision-making. Table 4.1 elaborates on various elements of FOL and examples.

4.1.1 Key Components of (FOL)

1. **Objects:**
   - Entities in the domain of discourse (e.g., people, places, things).
   - **Example**: "Socrates," "Athens," "Gold.", "Rama", "Bangalore", "Mercury"

Table 4.1 Basic First-Order Logic Elements

Element	Example
Constants	Numbers (1, 2, 3), Named objects (john, paris), Special values (π, e) Lakshmi, Jagannadh, cow
Variables	x, y, z, n - used as placeholders for values that can vary
Predicates	Parent(x,y) - "x is parent of y"
Functions	sqrt(x), average(x,y), sum(x,y), max(x,y)
Symbols	? (AND), ? (OR), ? (IMPLIES), ¬ (NOT), ? (IF AND ONLY IF)
Equality	= (equals), ? (not equals), = (less than or equal), = (greater than or equal)
Quantifiers	? (For all), ? (There exists)

2. **Predicates FOL:**
   - Represent relationships or properties of objects.
   - **Example:**
     - ❖ **Human**(Socrates): "Socrates is a human."
     - ❖ **LivesIn**(Socrates, Athens): "Socrates lives in Athens."
     - ❖ **LivesIn**(Rama, Bangalore): "Rama lives in Bangalore"

3. **Constants.:**
   - Specific objects in the domain.
   - **Example:** "Socrates," "Athens."

4. **Variables:**
   - Represent arbitrary elements in the domain
   - **Example**: x,y,z.

5. **Quantifiers. in FOL:**

   Enable reasoning about groups or subsets of objects:

   - **Universal Quantifier (∀\forall∀): "For all."**
     - ∀x Human(x): "All x are humans."
   - **Existential Quantifier (∃): "There exists."**
     - ∃ x LivesIn(x,Athens): "There exists an xxx who lives in Athens."
     - ∃x StudiesIn(x,Don Bosco Institute of Technology)

6. **Logical Connectives:**
   Same as in propositional logic: ¬, ∧, ∨, →, ↔

7. **DFS Functions:**
   Map objects to other objects.

   Example: ParentOf(x): "Parent of x."

   GrandParentOf(g,x)

Interpretation: "g" is the grandparent of x."

Here, g is the grandparent, and x is the grandchild.

This representation explicitly connects the grandparent and the grandchild.

Example: Using Parent Relationships:

If the grandparent relationship is derived from the parent relationship:

∃p (ParentOf(g,p)∧ParentOf(p,x))

- **Interpretation:**
  "There exists p such that g is the parent of p, and p is the parent of x."
- This representation explicitly defines a grandparent relationship in terms of intermediate parent relationships.

In table 4.2 summary for FOL logic components is presented.

Table 4.2 Summary for First-Order Logic Components

Component	Symbol	Name	Description	Example
Universal Quantifier	∀	For All	Asserts that a predicate is true for all elements in the domain	∀x (P(x))
Existential Quantifier	∃	There Exists	Asserts that there is at least one element in the domain for which the predicate is true	∃x (P(x))
Predicate	P(x)	Predicate	A function that returns true or false based on the object(s) it is applied to	P(x): "x is a person"
Conjunction	∧	AND	True if both predicates. are true	P(x) ∧ Q(x)
Disjunction	∨	OR	True if at least one of the predicates. is true	P(x) ∨ Q(x)
Negation	¬	NOT	True if the predicate is false	¬P(x)
Implication	→	IMPLIES	True if the first predicate implies the second predicate	P(x) → Q(x)
Biconditional	↔	BICONDITIONAL	True if both predicates. are either true or false	P(x) ↔ Q(x)

4.1.2 Representation Revisited

Representation revisited highlights the need to move beyond propositional logic to describe real-world situations more effectively. Propositional logic is limited to expressing simple true or false statements and cannot represent objects, their properties, or relationships between them. First Order Logic addresses these limitations by introducing objects, predicates, variables, functions, and quantifiers, allowing knowledge to be represented in a richer and more structured form. By explicitly modelling entities and their relationships, First Order Logic enables intelligent agents to reason about complex domains with greater precision and expressiveness.

For example, the statement "All students study Artificial Intelligence" can be represented in First Order Logic as ∀x (Student(x) → Studies (x, AI)), which cannot be directly expressed using propositional logic.

4.2 Syntax and Semantics. of First-Order Logic

The **syntax** defines the rules for constructing valid expressions in FOL. It specifies how symbols (constants, variables., predicates., connectives, quantifiers) can be combined.

Atomic Sentences

- **Predicates Applied to Terms:**
  - **Example**: Loves (Socrates, Philosophy): "Socrates loves philosophy."
  - **Loves** (Jagannadh, Artificial Intelligent Agents): Jagannadh loves Artificial Intelligent Agents

Breakdown of the Predicate

1. **Predicate Name:**
   - **Loves**: Represents the relationship of "loving."
2. **Arguments:**
   - **Jagannadh**: The subject (an individual or constant in the domain).
   - **Artificial Intelligent Agents**: The object being loved (a constant or entity in the domain).

3. **Interpretation:**
   - The predicate asserts that the relationship Loves holds between Jagannadh and Artificial Intelligent Agents.
   - It can be read as "Jagannadh loves Artificial Intelligent Agents."

Complex Sentences

1. **Formed Using Logical Connectives and Quantifiers:**
   - ❖ **Example**: $\forall x\ (Human(x) \rightarrow Mortal(x))$

"All humans are mortal."

4.2.1 Semantics. of First-Order Logic (FOL)

The semantics of First-Order Logic (FOL) defines the meaning of its symbols and sentences. It determines whether a sentence is true or false in a particular interpretation in FOL, providing a formal framework for understanding and reasoning about the relationships between objects in a domain.

4.2.2 Key Components of Semantics. in (FOL)

1. **Domain of Discourse:**
   - The domain is the set of all objects under consideration.
   - Every variable in FOL ranges over the domain.
   - **Example**:
     - ❖ **Domain**: All humans.
2. **Interpretation:**
   - An interpretation assigns meanings to the symbols used in FOL.
   - **Components of an interpretation include:**
     - ❖ **Constants**. in FOL: Mapped to specific objects in the domain.
     - ❖ **Example**: John → "John Smith."

- **Predicates Defined as relationships or properties over the domain.**
  - ❖ **Example**: Loves(x,y) True if x loves y.
- **Functions Maps elements of the domain to other elements.**
  - ❖ **Example**: Parent Of(x): Returns the parent of x.

3. **Atomic Sentences in FOL:**
   - An atomic sentence $P(t_1,t_2,..,t_n)$ is true if the relationship denoted by PPP holds for the objects denoted by $t_1,t_2,..,t_n$)
   - **Example**: Parent(John, Mary) is true if "John is the parent of Mary" in the given interpretation.

4. **Logical Connectives in FOL Semantics.:**
   - **The truth value of complex formulas depends on their connectives:**
     - ❖ $\neg\phi$: True if ϕ is false.
     - ❖ $\phi\wedge\psi$: True if both ϕ and ψ are true.
     - ❖ $\phi\vee\psi$: True if at least one of $\phi\psi$ true.
     - ❖ $\phi\rightarrow\psi$: True if ϕ or ψ is true.
     - ❖ $\phi\leftrightarrow\psi$: True if ϕ have the same truth value.

5. **Quantifiers.:**
   - **The meaning of a formula depends on the scope of quantifiers:**
     - ❖ **Universal Quantifier ($\forall$)**: $\forall x\phi(x)$is true if $\phi(x)$ is true for all x in the domain.
     - ❖ **Example**: $\forall x(\text{Human}(x)\rightarrow\text{Mortal}(x))$: True if every human in the domain is mortal.
     - ❖ **Existential Quantifier ($\exists$)**: $\exists x\phi(x)$ is true if $\phi(x)$ is true for at least one x in the domain.
     - ❖ **Example**: $\exists x\text{Loves}(x,\text{Mary})$: True if at least one individual loves Mary.

4.2.3 Examples of Semantics. in (FOL)

1. **Example 1: Simple Interpretation**
   - **Domain**: {Suryanaryana, Suryakanthammma, Kameswari
   - **Interpretation:**
     - ❖ **Loves**(x,y): True if x loves y.
     - ❖ **Loves**(Suryanarayana, Suryakanthamma) = True
2. **Sentence Evaluation:**
   - **Loves**(John,Mary): True (as defined in the interpretation).
   - **∃xLoves**(x,Mary): True (since John loves Mary)

Example 2: Quantifier Scope

3. **Sentence: ∀x∃yLoves(x,y):**
   - ❖ **Meaning**: "Everyone loves someone."
   - ❖ **Interpretation:** True if for every individual x, there exists at least one y such that Loves(x,y) is true.

Importance of Semantics. in (FOL)

1. **Consistency and Truth:**
   - Semantics**.** ensures that sentences are interpreted consistently based on the domain and interpretation.
   - This prevents ambiguities in reasoning.
2. **Knowledge Representation:**
   - FOL semantics allows precise representation of facts, rules, and relationships in AI systems.
3. **Automated:**
   - Semantics**.** underpins logical inference, enabling systems to deduce new facts from existing knowledge.
4. **Problem-Solving in FOL Semantics.:**
   - By defining clear semantics, FOL enables AI systems to solve problems involving constraints, relationships, and objectives.

5. **Natural Language Understanding:**
    - Mapping natural language to FOL requires an understanding of semantics to preserve meaning.

Summary: The semantics of First-Order Logic (FOL) form the basis for interpreting and evaluating logical sentences. By defining a domain, assigning meanings to constants, predicates., and functions, and using logical connectives and quantifiers, semantics ensures that FOL representations are meaningful and accurate/correct. This makes FOL an essential tool for reasoning, knowledge representation, and the creation of clever AI systems.

4.2.4 Using First Order Logic

Using First Order Logic involves applying its expressive power to represent knowledge and perform logical reasoning in intelligent systems. By using predicates, variables, quantifiers, and logical connectives, First Order Logic allows agents to describe objects, their properties, and relationships in a domain and to draw conclusions through inference mechanisms. It supports generalization and reasoning about classes of objects rather than individual instances, making it suitable for complex real-world applications such as knowledge-based systems and intelligent agents.

For example, from the statements ∀x (Human(x) → Mortal(x)) and Human (Socrates), an agent can infer Mortal (Socrates) using logical reasoning.

4.3 Inference. in First Order Logic: Propositional Versus First Order Inference:

Inference. in logic involves deriving new conclusions from a set of premises or facts using formal reasoning rules. In **First-Order Logic (FOL)**, inference extends the capabilities of propositional logic by incorporating objects, relationships, and quantifiers, making it more expressive and versatile.

This section explores the differences and capabilities of **propositional inference** versus **first-order inference**.

1. **Propositional Inference**.

Propositional inference operates on statements (propositions) that are either true or false. It is based on the rules of propositional logic and does not involve objects, quantifiers, or relationships.

Characteristics:

1. **Fid Propositions:**
   - Works with atomic propositions like P, Q, R, which represent fid truths.
   - **Example**: P: "It is raining.
2. **Inference. Rules:**
   - Inference. is performed using rules like Modus Ponens, Modus Tollens, and Resolution..
   - **Example (Modus Ponens):**
     - Premise 1: P→QP.
     - Premise 2: P.
     - Conclusion: Q.
3. **No Quantifiers.:**
   - Propositional logic cannot express statements involving "for all" (∀) or "there exists" (∃).
4. **Limited Expressiveness:**
   - Propositional inference cannot represent relationships between objects or handle dynamic scenarios effectively.
   - **Example**: Propositional logic cannot express "All humans are mortal."

2. **First-Order Inference**.

First-order inference extends propositional inference by incorporating objects, relationships, and quantifiers, enabling reasoning about structured knowledge.

Characteristics:

1. **Objects and Relationships:**
   - Works with predicates. like Human(x)or Loves(x,y), which represent properties or relationships.
   - **Example**: Mortal(x): "x is mortal."
2. **Quantifiers.:**
   - Uses universal quantifiers (∀) and existential quantifiers (∃\\ to express general or specific truths.
   - **Example**:
     - ∀x(Human(x)→Mortal(x)) "All humans are mortal."
     - **∃xLoves**(John,x): "John loves someone."
3. **Inference. Rules:**
   - Includes specialized inference techniques like unification, substitution, forward chaining, backward chaining, and resolution in the presence of quantifiers.
   - **Example(Unification):**
     - **Loves** (Johny) and Loves (John, Mary) Unified by y=Mary.
4. **Higher Expressiveness:**
   - First-order inference allows reasoning about dynamic, structured scenarios involving relationships, constraints, and complex conditions.

Propositional vs. First-Order Inference.:

Propositional inference deals with specific cases, while first-order inference generalizes and applies to broader domains. Table 4.3 elaborates the comparison of features between propositional and first-order inference.

Importance of First-Order Inference. in AI

1. **Expressiveness:**
    - Allows reasoning about structured knowledge involving objects, relationships, and quantifiers.

Table 4.3 Propositional Inference. and First-Order Inference

Feature	Propositional Inference.	First-Order Inference.
1. Nature and Expressiveness	Simple atomic statements; logical connectives (AND, OR, NOT, IF-THEN)	Predicates, quantifiers, variables., functions, constants; can express relationships and generalizations
2. Expressiveness and Limitations	Limited to specific facts; can't capture internal structure	Complex relationships and general rules; can't quantify over predicates.
3. Inference. Rules	Modus Ponens, Modus Tollens, Resolution.; Truth tables	Includes propositional rules plus Universal/Existential Instantiation and Generalization
4. Computational Complexity	NP-complete (SAT); generally, faster for small/medium problems	Undecidable in general; can be intractable for large domains
5. Decidability	Decidable and complete	Semi-decidable and incomplete (Gödel's theorems)
6. Knowledge Representation	Suitable for simple, specific facts; finite domains	Better for general knowledge, rules, complex relationships; infinite domains
7. Reasoning Capabilities	Limited to logical combinations of known facts	Can reason about classes of objects and general properties

8. Practical Applications	Circuit design, basic expert systems, SAT solvers	NLP, complex knowledge bases, automated theorem proving, planning
9. Learning Curve and Implementation	Easier to understand and implement	More advanced concepts; complex implementation
10. Inference. Algorithms	DPLL, CDCL for SAT solving	Resolution. with unification, Tableaux methods, Herbrand's theorem
11. Handling of Uncertainty	Can extend with probabilistic models; limited for general statements	Probabilistic first-order logics; better for complex, relational domains
12. Scalability	Good for limited propositions; can become unwieldy for many	Better for general rules; can handle infinite domains but may face computational challenges

2. **Abbreviations:**
   - **NP-complete SAT**: Non-deterministic Polynomial-time Complete Boolean Satisfiability Problem
   - **CDCL**: Conflict-Driven Clause Learning
   - **DPLL**: Davis-Putnam-Logemann-Loveland

3. **Scalability:**
   - Facilitates reasoning in complex, dynamic domains such as semantic web, natural language understanding, and knowledge graphs.

4. **Automation:**
   - Supports automated reasoning and knowledge discovery in AI systems.

5. **Generalization:**
   - Enables AI agents to generalize rules and apply them to new instances.

6. **Versatility:**
   - Essential for tasks like planning, theorem proving, and problem-solving in intelligent systems.

4.3.1 Specialized Inference. Techniques in First-Order Logic (FOL)

First-order inference encompasses various specialized techniques designed to handle the complexity of reasoning with quantifiers, predicates., and objects. These techniques—such as unification, substitution, forward chaining, backward chaining, and resolution—enable AI systems to effectively derive conclusions from structured knowledge. The following table provides a concise overview of these techniques, including their descriptions and examples, highlighting their relevance in AI agent contexts. In table 4.4 specialised techniques used in FOL is presented.

Table 4.4 Specialised Techniques used in (FOL)

Technique	Description	Example
Unification	A process of making two logical expressions identical by finding a suitable mapping of variables..	Unifying Loves (John, x) and Loves (John, Mary) results in x=Mary.
Substitution	Replacing variables. with constants or other terms in a logical formula based on a unifier.	Substituting x=Mary in Loves (John,x) gives Loves (John,Mary).
Forward Chaining	A data-driven inference method where rules are applied to known facts to derive new facts.	From Human (Socrates) and ∀x(Human(x)→Mortal(x)), infer Mortal (Socrates).
Substitution	Replacing variables. with constants or other	Substituting x=Mary in Loves (John,x)

	terms in a logical formula based on a unifier.	gives Loves (John, Mary).
Forward Chaining	A data-driven inference method where rules are applied to known facts to derive new facts.	From Human (Socrates) and ∀x(Human(x)→Mortal(x)), infer Mortal (Socrates).
Backward Chaining	A goal-driven inference method that starts with a query and works backward to find supporting facts.	To prove Mortal (Socrates) and ∀x(Human(x)→Mortal(x)).
Resolution.	A rule of inference for automated theorem proving, combining clauses to eliminate variables. and derive conclusions.	Resolving ¬Human (Socrates)∨Mortal (Socratess) with Human (Socrates) Mortal (Socrates).

4.4 Unification

Unification in Artificial Intelligence (AI) refers to the process of integrating multiple domains, such as computer vision, natural language processing, and robotics, into a cohesive framework. From a mathematical perspective, unification involves creating systems that generalise across tasks. In logic, unification plays a critical role, especially in first-order logic (FOL), where it is used to match formulas by finding common substitutions.

Unification Refers to Two Interconnected Concepts:

1. **Domain Integration**: The process of combining various AI domains—such as computer vision, natural language processing, robotics, and decision-making—into a cohesive framework. This approach aims to create systems capable of handling tasks across multiple cognitive domains, promoting generalization and interoperability.
2. **Logical Unification**: A mathematical process, particularly in **First-Order Logic (FOL)**, where formulas are matched by finding substitutions that make them identical. Logical unification

is fundamental to reasoning, automated theorem proving, and rule-based inference systems.

3. **Unification is a process of making two different logical atomic expressions identical by finding a substitution. Unification depends on the substitution process.**
4. **It takes two literals as input and makes them identical using substitution.**
5. **Let Ψ_1 and Ψ_2 be two atomic sentences and? be a unifier such that, Ψ_1? = Ψ_2?, then it can be expressed as UNIFY(Ψ_1, Ψ_2)**

Unification as Domain Integration

The goal of unification in AI is to move beyond specialized systems designed for narrow tasks (e.g., chatbots for conversation or algorithms for image recognition) and develop **general-purpose AI systems**. These systems integrate multiple domains into a unified architecture. capable of performing diverse tasks cohesively.

Key Features:

- **Multi-Task Learning**: A single system trained to perform tasks across domains, such as combining language understanding with visual perception.
- **General Intelligence**: Emulating human-like capabilities to perceive, reason, and act seamlessly across multiple contexts.
- **Interoperability**: Facilitating communication and data exchange between different AI systems to enhance overall functionality.

An AI system that can analyze an image, describe its content using natural language, and then decide actions based on the description (e.g., a robot navigating a room while describing obstacles).

Unification in Logical Systems

Logical unification in AI focuses on matching formulas in reasoning systems. It plays a critical role in **First-Order Logic (FOL)**, where the goal is to find substitutions for variables. that make logical expressions identical.

Key Features:

- **Matching Variables**: Ensuring predicates. or terms align by substituting variables. with constants or other terms.
- **Automated Reasoning**: Enabling logical inferences, theorem proving, and resolving queries in knowledge-based systems.

Example

- To unify Loves (Susheela) and Loves (Subbaiah), substitute x for Subbaiah and y with Susheela. Loves (Subbaiah and Susheela)

4.5 Forward Chaining

Forward chaining, also known as **forward deduction** or **forward reasoning**, is an inference method used in Artificial Intelligence (AI) to deduce new information from existing facts and rules. It is a **bottom-up approach** that starts with known facts and applies inference rules to derive new conclusions until a specific goal is reached. This method evaluates existing information—facts, derivations, and conditions—stored in the knowledge base and apply logical rules to infer additional facts or reach a decision. Forward chaining is commonly used in **expert systems** and other knowledge-driven AI applications. Figure 4.1 illustrates the forward chaining from facts to decision making by the AI system, namely agents.

How Forward Chaining Works

- **Input:** A set of known facts and a knowledge base of inference rules.

Process:

Evaluate facts and identify rules whose premises match these facts.

Apply those rules to infer new facts.

Repeat the process until no new facts can be deduced or a specific goal is achieved.

- **Output:** A conclusion or decision derived from the chain of logical inferences.

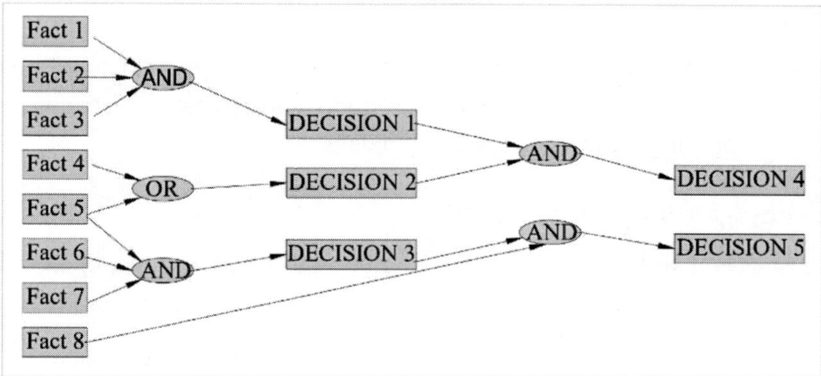

Figure 4.1 Forward Chaining

Example of Forward Chaining

Scenario:

- **Fact 1:** A dog is available for adoption through person A.
- **Fact 2:** Person B is looking to adopt a dog.
- **Inference. Rule:**

"If a dog is up for adoption and someone is looking to adopt, that person can adopt the dog."

Process:

a) **The system evaluates the known facts:**

- DogAvailable For A dog is available through A.
- LookingToAdopt(B): Person B is looking to adopt.

b) **The rule** DogAvailableForAdoption(x)∧LookingToAdopt(y)→ CanAdopt(y,x) matches the facts.

- The system applies the rule and infers:
- **Can A Dopt (B, A):** Person B can adopt the dog from person A.

Conclusion:

- Person B can adopt the dog from person A This demonstrates how forward chaining deduces new facts and reaches a decision by applying logical rules to known data.

Advantages of Forward Chaining

a) **Goal Independence**: Derives all possible conclusions, making it useful for exploring all consequences of a knowledge base.

b) **Simplicity**: Follows a straightforward, rule-driven approach.

c) **Applicability**: Ideal for systems with a large knowledge base requiring extensive fact exploration, such as medical diagnostics or decision-support systems.

Disadvantages of Forward Chaining

1. **Time-Consuming:**
   - Forward chaining can be computationally expensive because it evaluates all rules repeatedly, even if only a few are relevant. This makes it less efficient for large and complex knowledge bases.

2. **Data Synchronization:**
   - The need to synchronize large volumes of data can slow down the process, particularly when the knowledge base frequently changes or involves distributed systems.

3. **Unclear Fact Explanation:**
   - Forward chaining does not inherently explain *why* a conclusion was reached, as it focuses on generating new facts rather than providing justifications. This makes it less transparent compared to methods like backward chaining.

4. **Potential for Redundant Inferences:**
   - Forward chaining may repeatedly infer the same facts, wasting computational resources ***without contributing new insights.***

5. **Goal Irrelevance**
   - Since forward chaining explores all possible conclusions, it may infer facts that are unrelated to the intended goal, leading to inefficiency.

Addressing Disadvantages

While forward chaining has limitations, these can be mitigated by optimizing rule evaluation, prioritizing relevant facts, and integrating hybrid approaches that combine forward and backward chaining for more targeted reasoning.

4.6 Backward Chaining

Backward chaining, backward deduction, or backwards is a reasoning approach that works in the opposite/reverse direction as forward chaining. The approach that is top-down involves drawing judgments or setting objectives to get to the facts. Backward chaining is the process of backtracking usage in diagnostics, debugging, and prescriptions. Figure 4.2 illustrates the working of backward chaining.

- An inference technique that starts with a goal and works backward to see if existing facts and rules can support it. It asks questions based on the goal and searches for premises in rules that match known facts. If matches are found, the corresponding conclusions are added as temporary assumptions, potentially leading to other sub goals.
- **Example:**
  - ❖ **Goal**: "Is the floor wet?"
  - ❖ **Rule**: "The floor will be wet if it's raining and the windows are open."
  - ❖ The system asks if it's raining and checks if the windows are open. If both are true, the rule's conclusion ("The floor is wet") becomes a temporary assumption. Further reasoning might be needed to confirm or refute this assumption based on other rules and facts.

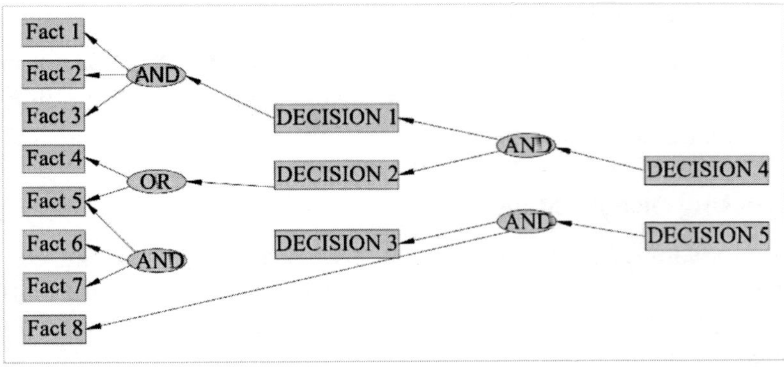

Figure 4.2 Backward Chaining

4.6.1 Advantages of Backward Chaining

1. **Focused Reasoning:**
   - Backward chaining is goal-oriented, allowing the system to focus only on the facts and rules relevant to achieving the specific goal.
2. **Efficiency for Specific Queries Efficiency of Backward Chaining:**
   - It avoids unnecessary exploration of unrelated facts, making it faster for targeted decision-making.
3. **Simpler Process for Known Goals:**
   - The process is straightforward when the endpoint or desired outcome is clearly defined.
4. **Effective Problem Solving:**
   - Backward chaining efficiently drives correct solutions by working systematically from the goal backward through supporting evidence.

4.6.2 Disadvantages Backward Chaining

1. **Single Answer:**
   - Backward chaining typically provides only one solution to the query, even if alternative solutions may exist.
2. **Less Flexibility:**
   - The method is rigidly tied to the defined goal, making it unsuitable for exploring a broad range of possibilities.

3. **Dependence on Known Endpoints Known Endpoints in Backward Chaining:**
    - It works best when the desired endpoint or conclusion is already known, limiting its applicability in open-ended problem-solving.
4. **Complex Execution:**
    - For large and complex knowledge bases, backward chaining can become challenging to execution due to the potential need for deep recursive searches.

4.6.3 Choosing Backward Chaining

Backward chaining is particularly well-suited for **diagnostic systems**, **planning tasks**, and **decision support tools**, where specific outcomes or conclusions are sought. While it is efficient and focused, its limitations make it less applicable to problems requiring exploration of multiple solutions or open-ended reasoning.

4.7 Resolution.

Resolution. is a powerful rule of inference used in **logic-based AI systems** to deduce new facts, resolve contradictions, and prove the validity of logical statements. It operates primarily in the context of **First-Order Logic (FOL)** and **Propositional Logic**, playing a central role in **automated theorem proving** and **logical reasoning**. Resolution simplifies complex logical expressions and is integral to the design of SAT solvers and knowledge-based systems.

4.7.1 Key Concepts of Resolution.

Proof by Contradiction:

Resolution. is based on the principle of proof by contradiction. To prove a hypothesis H, assume ¬H derive a contradiction (an empty clause ∅).

Clauses and Literals:

Resolution. operates on clauses, which are disjunctions of literals (atomic propositions or their negations).

Example: P∨¬QP is a clause with literals P and ¬Q.

Conjunctive Normal Form (CNF):

All logical expressions must be converted to CNF, where a formula is expressed as a conjunction of disjunctions.

Example: (P∨Q)∧(¬Q∨R).

Resolution. Rule:

The resolution rule combines two clauses that contain complementary literals to derive a new clause.

Example: From P∨QP and ¬Q∨R, resolve Q and ¬Qto derive P∨R.

Steps in Resolution.

Convert to CNF:

Rewrite the logical formula in Conjunctive Normal Form.

Negate the Hypothesis:

If proving H, assume ¬Hand add it to the clauses.

Apply the Resolution. Rule:

Iteratively resolve pairs of clauses to derive new clauses.

Check for Contradictions:

If an empty clause ∅is derived, the hypothesis H is proven true.

4.7.2 Example of Resolution. in AI

Problem:

Prove that Socrates is mortal using the following facts and rules:

Human (Jagannadh): "Jagannadh is human."

∀x (Human(x) → Mortal(x)): "All humans are mortal."

Steps:

Convert to CNF:

Human (Jagannadh): Already in CNF.

∀x(Human(x)→Mortal (x: Rewrite as ¬Human(x)∨Mortal(x).

Negate the Hypothesis:

Hypothesis: Mortal (Jagannadh).

Negate it: ¬Mortal (Jagannadh).

Apply Resolution.:

Clause 1: Human (Jagannadh).

Clause 2: ¬Human(x)∨Mortal(x) Mortal(x) (instantiate x=Jagannadh to get ¬Human (Jagannadh)∨Mortal (Jagannadh).

Clause 3: ¬Mortal (Jagannadh).

Resolve Human (Jagannadh) and ¬Human (Jagannadh)∨Mortal (Socrates: Mortal (Socrates).

Resolve Mortal (Socrates) and ¬Mortal (Socrates: ∅.

Conclusion:

The empty clause ∅ indicates a contradiction, proving that Socrates is mortal.

4.7.3 Applications of Resolution. in AI

1. **Automated Theorem Proving Theorem Proving in AI:**
   - Used to verify logical statements and prove mathematical theorems in systems like Coq, Prover9, and Isabelle.
2. **SAT Solvers:**
   - Integral to solving the Boolean Satisfiability Problem (SAT) in systems like DPLL and CDCL.
3. **Knowledge-Based Systems:**
   - Enables reasoning in expert systems by deriving new facts from existing knowledge bases.
4. **Logic Programming:**
   - Powers rule-based languages like Prolog to resolve queries using predefined rules and facts.
5. **Natural Language Processing (NLP) Resolution. in NLP:**
   - Facilitates reasoning about textual information by converting natural language statements into logical expressions.

6. **Constraint Satisfaction:**
    - Solves problems like scheduling and resource allocation by resolving constraints iteratively.

Advantages of Resolution.:

1. **Systematic and Complete:**
    - Guarantees a solution if one exists, making it reliable for refutation-based proofs.
2. **Uniform Representation:**
    - Operates on a standardized format (CNF), simplifying the inference process.
3. **Wide Applicability:**
    - Effective for both propositional and first-order logic, enabling its use across diverse AI applications.

Limitations of Resolution.

1. **Computational Complexity:**
    - Can be computationally expensive for large and complex problems due to clause explosion.
2. **Dependence on CNF:**
    - Converting logical formulas to CNF can increase the problem's size, complicating the reasoning process.
3. **Focus on Refutation:**
    - Works best for proving contradictions but does not inherently support constructive proofs or explanations.

Resolution. is a cornerstone of reasoning in AI, enabling systems to infer, validate, and deduce new knowledge systematically. Despite its computational challenges, its robustness and versatility make it indispensable for applications in theorem proving, SAT solving, knowledge-based systems, and beyond.

Chapter 4: Summary

This chapter presented **First Order Logic** as an advanced and expressive framework for knowledge representation and reasoning in Artificial Intelligence. It began by revisiting representation, showing how FOL overcomes the limitations of propositional logic by modelling environments in terms of objects, properties, and relationships. The use of variables and quantifiers allows FOL to express general rules and specific facts compactly and accurately.

The chapter explained the **syntax of First Order Logic**, detailing its fundamental components such as constants, variables, predicates, functions, logical connectives, and quantifiers. It also discussed the **semantics of FOL**, which define how logical expressions are interpreted over a domain of discourse and how truth values are assigned under a given interpretation or model. Together, syntax and semantics ensure precise and meaningful representation of knowledge.

Finally, the chapter focused on **inference in First Order Logic**, comparing it with propositional inference and introducing essential reasoning techniques. Concepts such as **unification** enable variable matching, while **forward chaining and backward chaining** support data-driven and goal-driven reasoning, respectively. The **resolution principle** was presented as a powerful and general inference method. These mechanisms enable AI systems to derive new knowledge, answer queries, and make logical decisions.

Conclusions

First Order Logic provides a strong theoretical and practical foundation for representing and reasoning about complex environments in Artificial Intelligence. By extending propositional logic with structured representations, FOL enables intelligent agents to reason about objects, relationships, and actions in a way that closely resembles human reasoning. Its well-defined syntax and semantics ensure clarity, consistency, and correctness in knowledge representation.

The inference techniques discussed in this chapter demonstrate how logical knowledge can be systematically exploited to draw conclusions and solve problems. Understanding these methods is essential for designing knowledge-based systems, expert systems, and reasoning engines. Overall, First Order Logic serves as a cornerstone of symbolic AI, bridging the gap between abstract logic and real-world intelligent behaviour.

Chapter – 5

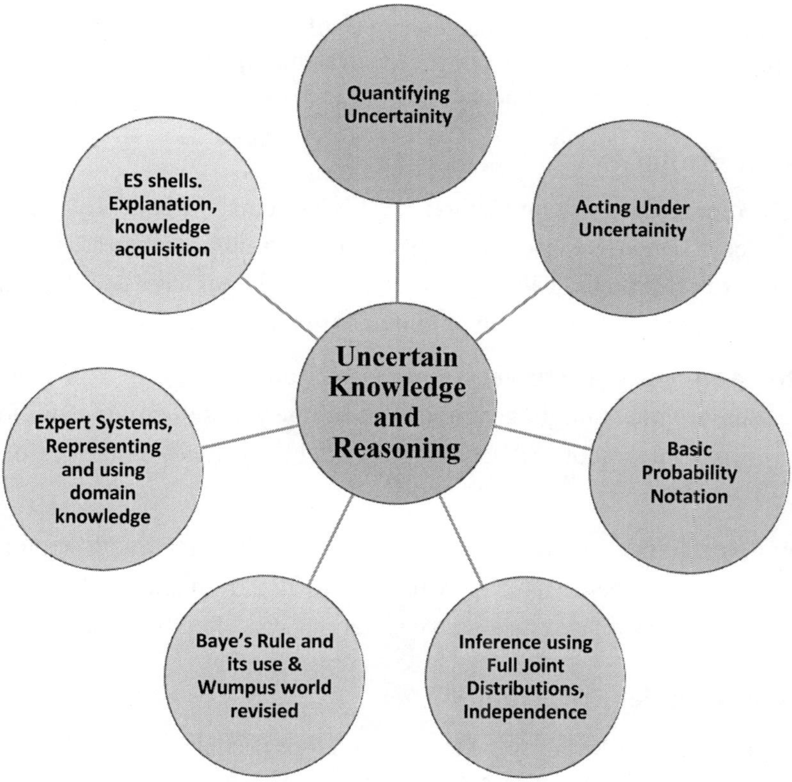
Quantifying Uncertainity
Acting Under Uncertainity
ES shells. Explanation, knowledge acquisition
Uncertain Knowledge and Reasoning
Expert Systems, Representing and using domain knowledge
Basic Probability Notation
Baye's Rule and its use & Wumpus world revisied
Inference using Full Joint Distributions, Independence

5.0 Introduction to Uncertain Knowledge and Reasoning

Uncertainty is an essential feature of real-world decision-making. AI systems often encounter partial/incomplete, unclear, or noisy information/data, making it impossible to operate with entirety certainty. In such situations, reasoning under uncertainty. becomes a vital aspect of creating intelligent systems capable of making reasonable choices.

This chapter explores the basic concepts of uncertain knowledge and reasoning, with a focus on how AI systems quantify and manage uncertainty. to make good decisions.

Why Uncertainty?

a) **Incomplete Knowledge**: AI systems frequently lack comprehensive information about the environment they are in. For example, a medical diagnosis system could not have access to all of the test results required to diagnose a condition.

b) **Ambiguity in Observations**: Data from sensors. or real-world environment might be ambiguous or noisy. A self-driving car, for instance, might fail to comprehend blurry road signals in bad weather.

c) Real-World Systems are complex and dynamic, with various interdependent factors. Creating a deterministic model that encompasses all conceivable situations can often be impractical.

Reasoning under Uncertainty

To reason under uncertainty., AI systems adopt probabilistic methods to represent and process uncertain knowledge. These methods allow the system to:

- Represent beliefs about unknown variables.
- Update these beliefs dynamically as new evidence becomes available.
- Make decisions that maximize expected utility., even with incomplete information.

5.1 Quantifying Uncertainty

In the real world, decision-making frequently involves incomplete, perplexing or noisy data. Humans regularly encounter unclear/unknown/ situations in which careful judgment is required to make sound decisions. Similarly, AI agents face uncertainty. when deciding on the best course of action to attain their objectives or desired outcomes.

Quantifying uncertainty. is thus an essential component of developing intelligent systems. Understanding and managing uncertainty helps artificially intelligent devices to make more informed and reliable decisions in complex environments. Uncertainty assessment and quantification are critical in developing robust and adaptive AI systems that can work effectively in the real world. Quantifying the response/action to be taken in uncertainty is a fundamental challenge in decision-making, artificial intelligence., and reasoning systems. This topic encompasses both quantifying uncertainty and the creation of strategies for achieving optimal conclusions in the absence of perfect information.

5.1.1 Uncertainty Arises Due to The Following Reasons

- **Incomplete data**: Not all relevant information is available.
- Noisy observations can be attributed by measurement or collection errors.
- **Inherent randomness**: Certain processes inherently stochastic.
- Quantifying uncertainty. enables AI and ML tasks to make better choices in such circumstances, enhancing reliability and adaptability.

5.1.2 Types of Uncertainty

Different types of uncertainty. must be considered:

- **Aleatory Uncertainty:**
  - Inherent randomness in a system. The data reveals/displays intrinsic unpredictability.
  - Cannot be reduced, even with infinite data.
  - For example, predicting the outcome of a dice throw or stock market fluctuations.

- **Epistemic Uncertainty:** Uncertainty due to limited knowledge. Due to lack of comprehension or information/data/facts.
  - Can be decreased with more data or better modelling strategies.
  - Suppose a model's uncertainty regarding the correct label for a rare class in a classification task.

Model uncertainty: Uncertainty in the mathematical representations used.

5.2 Acting under Uncertainty

When dealing with uncertainty., decision theory gives formal frameworks for making choices. The idea of maximum expected utility. implies that rational actors should select activities that maximize their expected utility:

In real-life situations, AI systems must make decisions using insufficient, ambiguous, or noisy information. Acting under uncertainty. is the process by which an intelligent agent chooses actions that maximize its chances of reaching/arriving at a desired end, even while it is unable to accurately forecasting the outcomes of those actions.

5.2.1 Why Uncertainty Arises in Decision-Making?

Uncertainty in decision-making stems from various factors:

- **Incomplete Information**: The agent lacks full knowledge of the environment.
  - **Example**: A robot navigating a new environment without a complete map.
- **Noisy Observations**: Data collected by sensors. or input devices may be imperfect.
  - **Example**: A self-driving car misinterpreting blurred road signs due to fog.
- **Dynamic Environments**: The world changes over time, making predictions difficult.
  - **Example**: Stock market fluctuations influenced by unforeseen events.

5.2.2 Key Principles of Acting under Uncertainty

1. **Quantifying Uncertainty**

   To act under uncertainty., an agent must first quantify the uncertainty. This is typically done using probability theory, which assigns likelihoods to different outcomes.

   - **Probability Distribution**: A mathematical representation of all possible outcomes and their probabilities.
   - **Example**: Predicting the probability of rain tomorrow based on historical weather data.

2. **Decision Theory**

   Decision-making under uncertainty. is guided by **Decision Theory**, which combines probabilities with utilities to evaluate the best course of action.

   Decision Theory = Probability Theory + Utility Theory

   Expected Utility: The agent selects the action that maximizes its expected utility:

$$EU(A) = \Sigma P(O_i|A) \cdot U(O_i) \qquad \text{........5.1}$$

Where:

- **$EU(A)$**: Expected utility. of action A.
- **$P(O_i|A)$**: Probability of outcome O_i given action A.
- **$U(O_i)$**: Utility (value) of outcome O_i.

3. **Trade-offs Between Risk and Reward**

   Agents must balance the potential rewards of an action with the risks associated with uncertainty. Risk-Averse and Risk-Tolerant Agents.

- **Risk-Averse Agents**: Prefer safer actions with lower variance in outcomes.
- **Risk-Tolerant Agents**: opt for actions with higher potential rewards, even if they involve greater risk.
- **Example**: A robot choosing between a known, longer path and an unknown, shorter path.

4. **Bayesian Decision-Making**

   Bayesian reasoning helps agents update their beliefs about the environment as new evidence becomes available. This is crucial for refining decisions over time.

   - **Example**: A medical diagnosis system adjusts the probability of a disease as test results are observed.

5.2.3 Summarizing Uncertainty

Uncertainty arises naturally in everyday life due to partial knowledge, complexity, or randomness in data and processes. Understanding and addressing the reasons of uncertainty. is crucial in AI and ML as it enables systems to make more informed and logical decisions. This section addresses the primary causes of uncertainty: laziness, theoretical ignorance, and practical ignorance, along with the implications of decision-making. Summarizing Uncertainty

Uncertainty is an inherent aspect of real-world environments where AI agents operate. It arises due to factors such as incomplete knowledge, noisy observations, and the inherent randomness of certain events. Quantifying and reasoning about uncertainty. allows AI agents to make informed decisions even when the information is ambiguous or incomplete.

In AI, uncertainty. is represented and managed using tools like probability theory and Bayes' Rule. These tools enable agents to update their beliefs based on new evidence, infer missing information, and make rational decisions under uncertainty. By leveraging independence. assumptions, full joint distributions, and decision theory, engineers can simplify the modelling of uncertainty and design robust systems. This ability to quantify, summarize, and act under uncertainty is critical for applications ranging from autonomous vehicles to medical diagnosis systems. Figure

5.1 depicts Sources of uncertainty arising from laziness, practical ignorance, and theoretical ignorance.

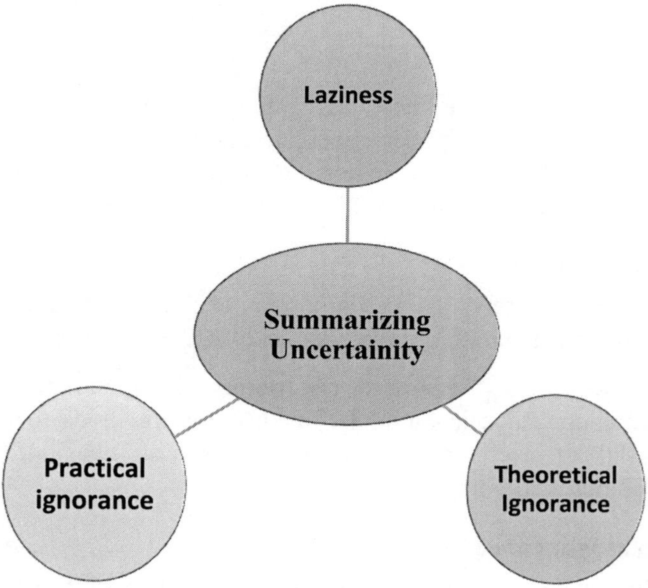

Figure 5.1 Sources of Uncertainty Arising from Laziness, Practical Ignorance, and Theoretical Ignorance

1. Laziness

Definition: Laziness denotes the difficulty and effort required for building complete rules and models which account for every possible situation/use case.

- **Explanation**: Creating an exhaustive list of antecedents (conditions) and consequents (outcomes) for every case might not be feasible in some fields of study. Ensuring that rules are exception less—valid in all situations—requires significant effort and time.
- Diagnosing diseases is challenging due to patient diversity, making it impossible to list all probable symptoms and their implications.
- **Impact on AI**: To avoid comprehensive modelling, systems must employ approximate rules or heuristic methods that accept some degree of uncertainty.. Probabilistic techniques and machine learning are used to successfully control incompleteness.

2. Theoretical Ignorance

Definition: Theoretical ignorance arises when there is no complete or commonly accepted theory for a certain subject of knowledge.

Explanation

- In fields like medicine and study of climate, incomplete comprehension of basic processes can create gaps in theoretical models. The reason why Medical science's incomplete understanding of diseases, like Alzheimer's, necessitates

3. Impact on AI

AI systems to rely on partial/incomplete theories and unclear probabilities when predicting outcomes or suggesting treatments.

- AI agents must adapt to uncertainty. by using probabilistic reasoning, Bayesian models, or ensemble methods to integrate partial theories and update predictions as new information becomes available.

4. Practical Ignorance

Practical ignorance is the inability to obtain every piece of data needed to make informed choices, regardless of whether a theoretical framework exists.

Explanation

- Practical constraints, such as cost, time, and feasibility, might restrict gathering data.

Example:

A doctor may suspect a medical condition but not be able to confirm it due to high costs or the inadequate availability of tests for diagnosis.

Impact on AI

AI systems use probabilistic methods and inference to fill gaps and forecast outcomes. Probability provides a way of summarizing the uncertainty that comes from our laziness and ignorance, thereby solving the qualification problem.

Approaches to Acting under Uncertainty

1. Probabilistic Models

Use probability distributions to model uncertainty. in outcomes. Examples include:

- Bayesian Networks
- Hidden Markov Models

2. Reinforcement Learning

Agents learn optimal actions by exploring an environment and receiving feedback. This approach is particularly effective in dynamic and uncertain environments.

3. Heuristic Methods

Simplified rules or approximations used when exact calculations are impractical.

- **Example**: A chess-playing AI evaluating moves based on experience rather than exhaustively calculating all possibilities.

5.3 Basic Probability Notation

Probability theory is a cornerstone of Artificial Intelligence (AI) and Machine Learning (ML), especially when dealing with uncertainty.. This section introduces basic probability notations and concepts that form the foundation for understanding probabilistic reasoning, Bayesian inference, and machine learning models. In Artificial Intelligence and Machine Learning contexts, uncertainty is handled using probability theory. To use probability concepts effectively, certain basic symbols and terms must be understood. These notations help describe all possible outcomes of an uncertain situation. The first such concept is the *sample space*.

a) Sample Space (Ω)

The sample space is the set of all possible outcomes of a random experiment. It is denoted by Ω(Omega)

- **Example**: In the case of a coin toss, $\Omega = \{\text{Heads, Tails}\}$.
- For rolling a six-sided die, $\Omega = \{1, 2, 3, 4, 5, 6\}$.

b) Events (A, B, C,...)

An **event** is a subset of the sample space, representing a specific outcome or a group of outcomes of interest. Events are typically denoted by capital letters such as A, B, C, etc.

- **Example: For a die roll, the event A (rolling an even number) is A={2, 4, 6}**
- **Similarly rolling an odd number another event B is**
- **B={1, 3, 7}**

c) **Probability of an Event P(A)**

The **probability of an event** is a measure of the likelihood of the event occurring. It is denoted by P(A) and satisfies the following properties:

$$0 \leq P(A) \leq 1$$

$P(\Omega)=1$ (The probability of the entire sample space is 1).

For mutually exclusive events A and B, $P(A \cup B)=P(A)+P(B)$ = $P(A) + P(B)$.Figure 5.2 illustrates the concept of probability of an Event say **A**

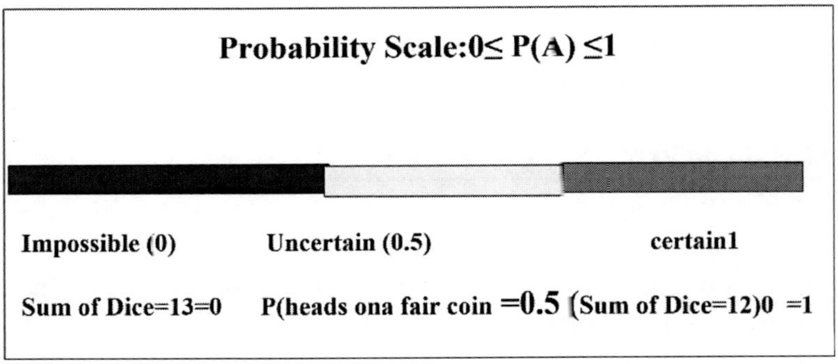

Figure 5.2 Probability of an Event Scale

d) **Complement of an Event (A^c)**

The **complement** of an event A, denoted $\mathbf{A^c}$ (Figure 5.3 (e)) is the set of outcomes in the sample space that are not in A.

$$P(A^c)=1-P(A)$$

- **Example**: If A is rolling a 4 on a die, A^c = {1, 2, 3, 5, 6}.

e) **Union of Events (A∪B)**

The **union** of two events A and B, denoted A∪B (Figure 5.3 (c)), is the event that either A or B (or both) occur.

$$P(A \cup B) = P(A)+P(B)-P(A \cap B)$$

f) Intersection of Events (A∩B)

The **intersection** of two events A and B, denoted A∩B A (Figure 5.3 (d)), is the event that both A and B occur simultaneously.

P(A∩B)=P(A)·P(B|A)

Where P(B|A) is the conditional probability of B given A.

g) Independent Events

Two events A and B are said to be **independent** if the occurrence of one does not affect the occurrence of the other.

P(A∩B)=P(A)·P(B)

- **Example**: Tossing two coins: The result of the first coin does not affect the second coin.

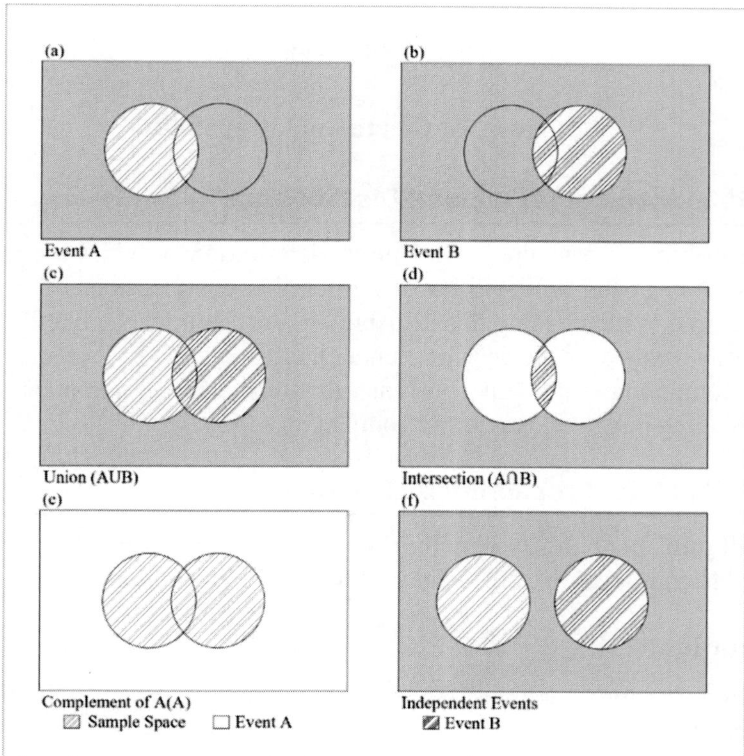

Figure 5.3 Sample Space, Events, Their Complements, Unions, Intersections, and Independent Events

Conditional Probability (P(B|A))

The **conditional probability** of event B given event A, denoted P(B|A), is the probability that B occurs given that A has occurred illustrated in Figure 5.4.

$$P(B|A) = P(A \cap B) / P(A), P(A) > 0$$

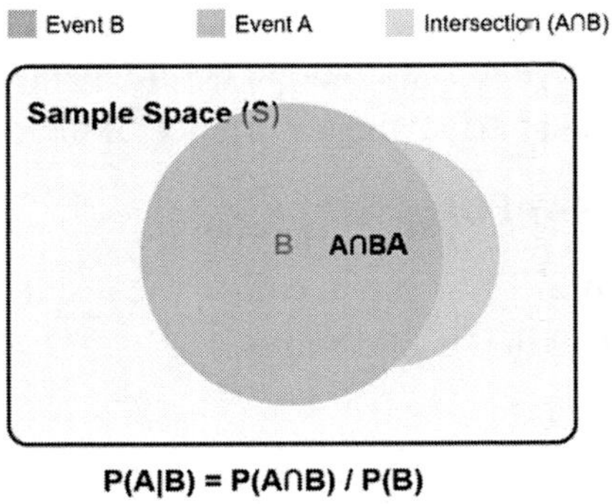

Figure 5.4 Conditional Probability

5.4 Inference. using Full Joint Distributions

In probabilistic reasoning, a **full joint distribution** provides a complete description of the probabilities of all possible combinations of variable values in a system. Using this distribution, we can infer the likelihood of specific events or make decisions under uncertainty.. However, managing and computing with full joint distributions can be computationally challenging due to their size and complexity.

5.4.1 Full Joint Probability Distribution

A **full joint probability distribution** represents the probability of every possible combination of the values of multiple random variables..

Definition:

Given n random variables. $X_1, X_2, \ldots, X_n$, the full joint distribution is defined as:

$$\mathbf{P(X_1, X_2, \ldots, X_n)}$$

This describes the probability of each possible combination of $X_1, X_2, \ldots, X_n$

Example:

For two binary variables., X (Rain: Yes/No) and Y (Traffic: Heavy/Light), the joint distribution is presented in table 5.1:

Table 5.1 Joint distribution two variables. X(Rain) and B(Traffic)

X (Rain)	Y (Traffic)	P (X, Y)
Yes	Heavy	0.3
Yes	Light	0.2
No	Heavy	0.4
No	Light	0.1

Key Concepts in Using Full Joint Distributions

1. Marginalization

Marginalization is the process of summing out one or more variables. from the joint distribution to compute the probability of other variables.

Formula:

For two variables. X and Y, the marginal probability of X is:

$$P(X) = \sum_{Y} P(X, Y) \quad \text{...........5,2}$$

From the above table 5.1:

P(Rain = Yes) = P(Rain = Yes, Traffic = Heavy) + P(Rain = Yes, Traffic = Light) = 0.3 + 0.2 = 0.5

5.5 Independence in Relation to Quantifying Uncertainty

Independence is a powerful concept in probability theory that simplifies the representation and computation of joint distributions. When two or more variables. are independent, the joint probability distribution of those variables can be factored into smaller, manageable components. This principle is especially useful in AI agent development, where large, complex environments with numerous variables must be modelled efficiently. By leveraging independence., AI agent developers can reduce computational complexity, making it feasible to reason and make decisions under uncertainty.. Below are two examples illustrating how independence simplifies joint distributions in practical scenarios?

Figure 5.5 illustrates how independence allows a joint probability distribution to be decomposed into smaller, simpler distributions.

Examples of Independence

Weather and Dental Problems Are Independent

Scenario:

Suppose an AI healthcare assistant needs to predict the likelihood of a patient having dental problems and bad weather on the same day.

Assumption:

The variables. Weather (e.g., W: Rainy or Sunny) and Dental Problems (e.g., D: Present or Absent) are independent because the weather conditions do not influence dental health.

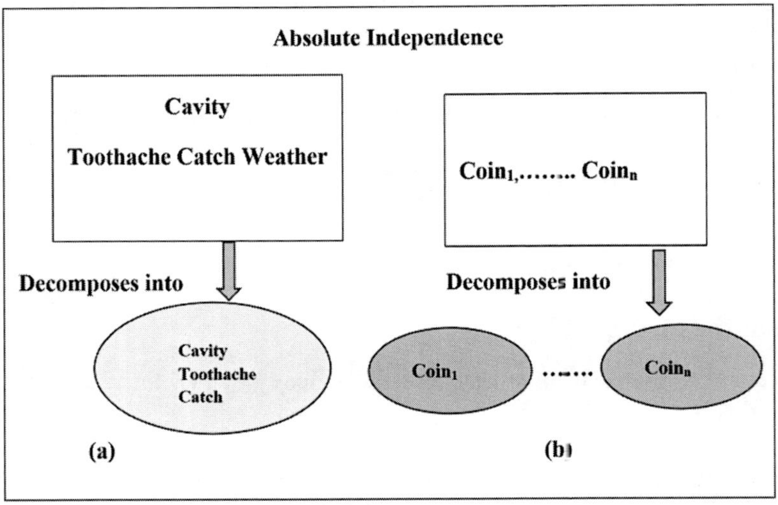

Figure 5.5 Decomposing Joint Probability Distributions Using Independence

Two examples of factoring a large joint distribution into smaller distributions, using absolute independence.. (a) Weather and dental problems are independent. (b) Coin flips are independent.

Joint Distribution:

If W and D are independent, their joint probability can be factored as:

$$P(W, D) = P(W) \cdot P(D) \quad \text{.................5.3}$$

Simplification:

Instead of calculating and storing probabilities for all combinations of W and D (e.g., Rainy + Present, Rainy + Absent, Sunny + Present, Sunny + Absent), we can store just the marginal probabilities P(W) and P(D).

Implications for AI Agent. Development:

- Saves computational resources by reducing the size of the distribution.
- Allows modular reasoning, where weather predictions and dental health predictions can be handled independently.

Coin Flips Are Independent

Scenario:

Consider an AI system simulating coin flips to predict outcomes. Let $X_1, X_2, \ldots, X_n$ represent the outcomes of **n** coin flips.

Assumption:

Each coin flip is independent of the others, meaning the outcome of one flip does not influence the outcome of another.

Joint Distribution:

The joint probability of observing a sequence of outcomes X1, X2,...,Xn is the product of the individual probabilities:

$$P(X_1, X_2, \ldots, X_n) = P(X_1) \cdot P(X_2) \cdot \cdots \cdot P(X_n)$$

Simplification:

Instead of storing 2^n entries for all possible combinations of outcomes, the system only needs to store the probability of a single coin flip (e.g., P(Heads)=0.5, P(Tails)=0.5.

Implications for AI Agent. Development

Facilitates simulations and predictions involving large numbers of coin flips or similar independent events.

Supports scalability in probabilistic modelling for games, gambling applications, or stochastic simulations.

Role of Independence in AI Agent. Development

a) **Efficiency in Computation:** Independence simplifies joint distributions, reducing storage and computational requirements. This is critical for real-time applications where speed and resource efficiency are essential.

b) **Modular Problem-Solving:** Independence allows separate modelling of unrelated variables., enabling modular reasoning. For instance, in multi-agent systems, agents can operate independently unless explicitly coordinated.

c) **Scalability:** Factoring distributions using independence. supports scalability, allowing agents to handle large numbers of variables. in complex environments.

d) **Improved Decision-Making:** Independence assumptions help focus computational efforts on interdependent variables., improving decision-making efficiency without sacrificing accuracy.

By exploiting independence., AI developers can design agents capable of quantifying uncertainty. efficiently. Whether modelling unrelated phenomena like weather and dental health or simulating independent events like coin flips, independence simplifies probabilistic reasoning and enables robust agent design in complex, uncertain environmen

5.6 Bayes' Rule and its Uses

Reasoning under uncertainty is a fundamental requirement for intelligent systems. In many real-world situations, an AI agent does not have complete information about the environment and must update its beliefs as new evidence becomes available. Bayes' Rule provides a principled mathematical framework for revising beliefs in light of new evidence and lies at the heart of probabilistic reasoning in Artificial Intelligence.

5.6.1 Bayes' Rule

Bayes' Rule describes the relationship between prior knowledge, new evidence, and updated belief. It is derived from the basic definition of conditional probability.

*This is **Bayes***

$$P(A|B) = P(B|A) \times P(A) / P(B) \quad \text{.............5.4}$$

Terminology

- **P(A|B)**: Posterior probability (what we want to find)
- **P(B|A)**: Likelihood (probability of evidence given hypothesis)
- **P(A)**: Prior probability (our initial belief about A)
- **P(B)**: Marginal probability or evidence (normalizing constant)

It should be noted with the emphasis, that Bayes' Rule is not merely a formula but a rational method of belief updating. The key idea is:

New evidence should modify existing beliefs in a logically consistent way.

- The prior represents background knowledge.
- The likelihood captures how well the hypothesis explains the evidence.
- The posterior represents the revised belief after observing evidence.

Thus, Bayes' Rule enables an agent to combine knowledge from the past with current observations.

5.6.2 Simple Illustrative Example

Consider a medical diagnosis problem where uncertainty must be handled using probability:

Given That,

- 1% of a population has a disease.
- A test detects the disease correctly 99% of the time.
- The test gives a false positive 5% of the time.

Let:

- **A**: The patient has the disease
- **B**: The test result is positive

Given Information:

- $P(A)=0.01$
  (Only 1% of the population has the disease — prior probability)
- $P(B|A)=0.99$
- (The test correctly detects the disease 99% of the time — likelihood)
- $P(B|\neg A)=0.05$
- (The test gives a false positive 5% of the time)

Step 1: Compute the Evidence P(B)

$P(B)=P(B|A)P(A)+P(B|\neg A)P(\neg A)$

$P(B)=(0.99)(0.01)+(0.05)(0.99)=0.0099+0.0495=0.0594$

Step 2: Apply Bayes' Rule

$$P(A \mid B) = \frac{P(B \mid A)P(A)}{P(B)}$$

$$P(A \mid B) = \frac{0.99 \times 0.01}{0.0594} \approx 0.167$$

............5.5

Interpretation

Even though the test is highly accurate, the probability that the patient actually has the disease given a positive test result is only about **16.7%**. This result highlights an important idea emphasized.

5.6.3 Why Bayes' Rule is Important in AI and ML?

Bayes' Rule is central to many AI and ML techniques because it allows systems to deal with uncertainty in a structured manner.

1. **Learning from Data**

In Bayesian learning, model parameters are treated as random variables. As new data arrives, Bayes' Rule updates the probability distribution over these parameters.

2. **Classification**

Naïve Bayes classifiers use Bayes' Rule to compute the probability of each class given the observed features and choose the class with the highest posterior probability.

3. **Perception and Diagnosis**

Bayesian inference is widely used in speech recognition, medical diagnosis, and fault detection, where observations are noisy and uncertain.

4. **Decision Making Under Uncertainty**

Bayes' Rule helps agents evaluate possible explanations for observed events and choose actions that maximize expected utility..

5.6.4 Bayesian Inference

Bayesian inference refers to the general process of applying Bayes' Rule repeatedly as more evidence becomes available. An intelligent agent continuously updates its beliefs as it interacts with the environment, leading to more accurate and informed decisions over time. It should be noted that, Bayesian inference provides a **normative standard**—that is, it defines how a rational agent *should* reason under uncertainty.

5.7 Wumpus World Revisited

The Wumpus World provides a simple yet powerful framework for illustrating how an intelligent agent reasons under uncertainty. In earlier chapters, the Wumpus World was introduced using propositional logic, where the agent made definite true or false conclusions based on percepts. However, real-world environments are rarely so precise. Sensors may be noisy, perceptions may be incomplete, and actions may have uncertain outcomes. Revisiting the Wumpus World allows us to apply probabilistic reasoning to handle such uncertainty more realistically.

In the probabilistic version of the Wumpus World, percepts such as breeze and stench are treated as uncertain evidence rather than absolute facts. The agent represents its knowledge using probabilities and updates its beliefs about the presence of pits or the Wumpus using Bayes' Rule. This requires defining a joint probability distribution over relevant variables and exploiting independence assumptions to make inference computationally feasible.

By quantifying uncertainty, the agent can evaluate the likelihood of danger in adjacent squares and act under uncertainty by choosing actions that maximize expected utility. rather than guaranteeing safety. Thus, the Wumpus World revisited serves as a unifying example that brings together the key ideas of this chapter—probability notation, inference, independence, and Bayesian updating—demonstrating how rational agents reason and act in uncertain environments.

5.7.1 Comparison: Logical vs. Probabilistic Agents

Table 5.2 provides a comparison of logical and probabilistic agents in various aspects related to an environment.

Table 5.2 Comparison: Logical vs. Probabilistic Agents

Aspect	Logical Agent	Probabilistic Agent
Knowledge representation	True/False/Unknown	Degrees of belief (0 to 1)
Decision criterion	Provably safe	Acceptable risk level
Performance	Overly cautious	Optimal given information
Flexibility	Limited to certain knowledge	Handles uncertainty naturally
Exploration	May get stuck	Can take calculated risks

This comparison demonstrates why probabilistic agents, by balancing risk and reward, achieve better performance in the Wumpus World than logical agents that require complete certainty.

Performance Comparison

Scenario: Breeze detected, two possible pit locations.

- **Logical Agent**: Cannot proceed (both unsafe, cannot prove which)
- **Probabilistic Agent**: Chooses square with lower pit probability

Thus, the probabilistic formulation of the Wumpus World enables agents to act rationally under uncertainty, leading to better overall performance than strictly logical agents.

5.8 Expert Systems

Expert Systems (ES) are one of the earliest and most successful applications of Artificial Intelligence. They are designed to **emulate the decision-making ability of a human expert** in a specific domain such as medicine, engineering, finance, or agriculture. Instead of solving problems through general intelligence., expert systems rely on **domain-specific knowledge** and **logical or** probabilistic **reasoning** to provide advice, diagnosis, or decisions.

5.8.1 Representing and Using Domain Knowledge

Domain Knowledge

Domain knowledge refers to **specialized facts, rules, and heuristics** related to a particular field. For example:

- Medical domain → symptoms, diseases, treatments
- Mechanical domain → faults, causes, repair actions
- Agriculture domain → soil type, crops, fertilizers

Knowledge Representation in Expert Systems

Expert systems store domain knowledge in a **Knowledge Base (KB)** using suitable representation techniques. Table 5.3 provides a comparison of Common Knowledge Representation Methods.

Table 5.3 Common Knowledge Representation Methods

Rule-based representation	Uses IF–THEN rules	IF fever AND cough THEN flu
Facts	Simple assertions	Temperature = High
Frames	Structured objects with slots	Disease frame with symptoms
Probabilistic rules	Handles uncertainty	IF cough THEN flu (0.7)

Using Domain Knowledge

The **Inference Engine** applies reasoning techniques (forward or backward chaining) on the knowledge base to derive conclusions.

Example

IF engine_not_starting AND battery_dead

THEN replace_battery

Here, the system reasons like a human technician.

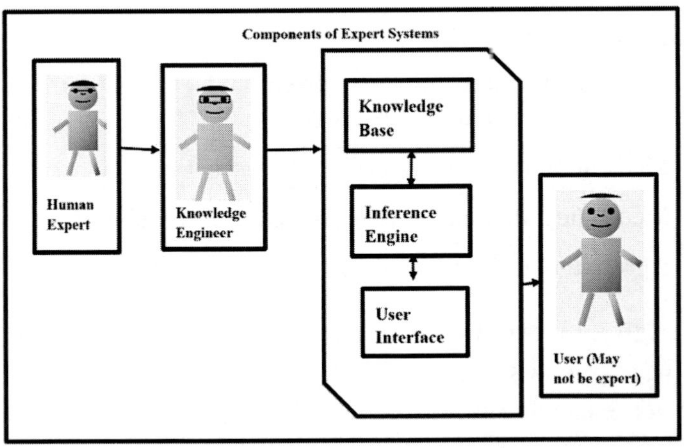

Figure 5.6 Basic Architecture of an Expert System

(Expert Systems – Image generated using Free AI Image Generator: Text to Image Online)

Title: *Architecture of an Expert System Showing Knowledge Base and Inference Engine*

Figure 5.6 illustrates the basic architecture. of an expert system. The **Knowledge Base** stores domain-specific facts and rules obtained from human experts. The **Inference Engine** applies logical and probabilistic reasoning techniques to the knowledge base to derive conclusions or recommendations. The **User Interface** enables interaction between the user and the system, allowing users to input queries and receive advice. The **Explanation Facility** provides justifications for the system's conclusions, enhancing transparency and user confidence. The **Knowledge Acquisition Module** supports the process of capturing, updating, and refining expert knowledge within the system.

5.8.2 Expert System Shells ES Shells

An **Expert System Shell** is a **generic expert system framework without domain knowledge**. It provides the tools required to build expert systems, while the developer only needs to add the specific knowledge.

Key Components of an ES Shell

- Inference engine
- Knowledge representation mechanism
- User interface
- Explanation facility

Why Use Expert System Shells?

- Faster development
- No need to design reasoning mechanisms from scratch
- Easy maintenance and updating of knowledge

Table 5.4 Compares the Expert System and Expert System Shell

Feature	Expert System	Expert System Shell
Domain knowledge	Included	Not included
Inference engine	Fid	Provided
Customization	Limited	High
Development time	Long	Short
Reusability	Low	High

An **Expert System** is a complete application that includes a knowledge base containing domain-specific facts and rules, an inference engine, and a user interface designed to solve a particular problem. In contrast, an **Expert System Shell** is a generalized software framework that provides the inference engine, user interface, and explanation facility but does not include domain knowledge. The knowledge base must be added separately to create a specific expert system. Expert system shells simplify development by allowing new expert systems to be built by only changing the knowledge base. Figure 5.7 illustrates how an Expert System Shell provides a generic inference engine, user interface, and explanation facility, which become a complete expert system when domain-specific knowledge is added to the knowledge base.

Expert System with Expert Shell System

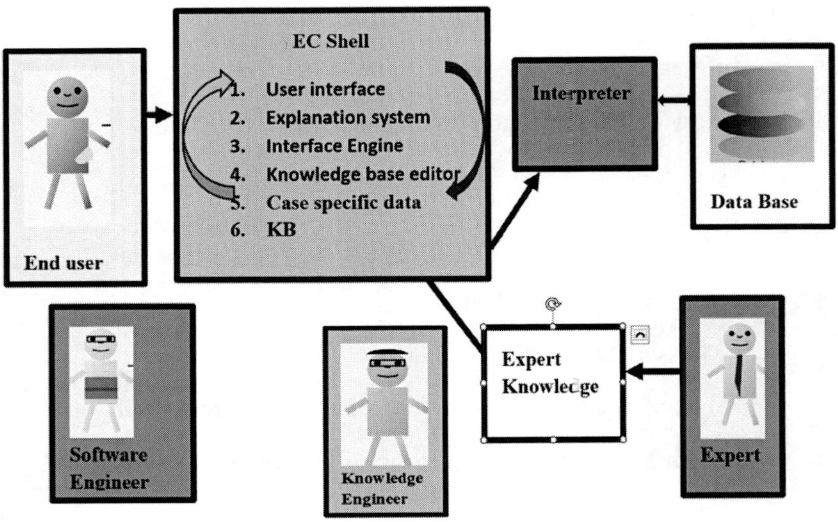

Figure 5.7 Expert Systems with Expert System Shell

5.8.3 Explanation Facility

One important feature of expert systems is the **explanation facility**, which allows the system to explain:

- **Why** a particular question was asked
- **How** a conclusion was reached

Importance of Explanation

- Builds user trust
- Helps in learning and validation
- Essential in domains like medicine and law

Example Explanation

"The system concluded malaria because the patient has fever, chills, and recent travel history."

5.8.4 Knowledge Acquisition

Knowledge acquisition is the process of **collecting, organizing, and encoding expert knowledge** into the system.

Sources of Knowledge

- Human experts
- Textbooks and manuals
- Case studies
- Databases

Knowledge Acquisition Methods

Knowledge Acquisition is the process of extracting knowledge from various sources and converting it into a form that an expert system can understand and use.

- **Interviews:**

  Knowledge engineers interact directly with domain experts to obtain facts, rules, and problem-solving strategies.

- **Observation:**

  Experts are observed while they solve real problems, helping identify implicit knowledge that may not be easily verbalized.

- **Questionnaires:**

  Structured sets of questions are used to systematically collect knowledge from one or more experts in a consistent manner.

- **Machine Learning:**

  Algorithms automatically learn patterns, rules, or models from historical data, reducing reliance on manual knowledge extraction.

The table5.5 summarizes the major ***knowledge acquisition methods*** *used to capture and formalize expert knowledge for building effective expert systems.*

The following table5.5 presents various ***knowledge acquisition methodologies*** *used to formalize expert knowledge for building effective expert systems.*

Table 5.5 Various Knowledge Acquisition Methodologies

Method	Description
Interviews	Direct discussion with domain experts
Observation	Watching experts while they solve problems
Questionnaires	Structured collection of expert knowledge
Machine Learning	Automatically learning rules and patterns from data

Knowledge Acquisition Bottleneck

Acquiring accurate and complete knowledge is difficult, time-consuming, and often referred to as the **knowledge acquisition bottleneck** Human experts may find it hard to explain their reasoning clearly, and translating this knowledge into formal rules or models is complex. This bottleneck is one of the major challenges in developing and maintaining expert systems.

5.8.5 Simple Example of an Expert System

Medical Diagnosis Expert System

Symptom	Value
Fever	Yes
Headache	Yes
Body pain	Yes

Rule

IF fever AND headache AND body pain

THEN diagnosis = viral fever

The system reasons using stored rules and provides a diagnosis along with an explanation.

Key Takeaways

- Expert systems simulate **human expert reasoning**
- Domain knowledge is stored in a **knowledge base**
- ES shells simplify expert system development
- Explanation facilities improve **transparency and trust**
- Knowledge acquisition is a **critical and challenging task**

Chapter 5: Summary

In real-world environments, intelligent agents rarely operate with complete, accurate, or certain information. Chapter 5 addresses this challenge by introducing **uncertain knowledge and reasoning**, emphasizing how intelligent systems can make rational decisions despite incomplete data and unpredictable outcomes Moving beyond the assumption of certainty used in earlier chapters, this chapter treats uncertainty as an inherent and unavoidable aspect of intelligent behaviour.

The chapter begins with **acting under uncertainty**, explaining why deterministic and purely logical reasoning is insufficient for many AI applications. Real-world sensors may produce noisy data, environments can change dynamically, and the results of actions are often probabilistic rather than guaranteed. To handle such conditions, intelligent agents must reason using **probability theory**, which allows them to represent beliefs in terms of likelihoods instead of absolute true or false values.

Next, the chapter introduces **basic probability concepts and notation**, including random variables, probability distributions, conditional probability, and joint probability distributions. These concepts provide a formal and mathematical foundation for representing uncertainty and form the basis for probabilistic inference in artificial intelligence. systems.

The process of **inference using full joint probability distributions** is then explored. While a complete joint distribution allows an agent to compute the probability of any hypothesis or event, the chapter highlights the practical limitations of this approach due to the exponential growth in complexity as the number of variables increases. To address this issue, the chapter discusses **independence and conditional independence**, which enable the simplification of probabilistic models and more efficient reasoning.

A key focus of the chapter is **Bayes' Rule**, which provides a systematic method for updating an agent's beliefs when new evidence becomes available. Through Bayes' Rule, prior knowledge is combined with observed data to produce posterior probabilities, allowing intelligent agents to learn from experience and adapt their behaviour over time.

The chapter also revisits the **Wumpus World**, extending the earlier logical formulation to a **probabilistic version**. In this setting, the agent reasons about the likelihood of pits and the Wumpus rather than relying on definite conclusions. This example clearly illustrates how probabilistic reasoning enables more realistic and robust decision-making in uncertain environments.

Expert Systems was introduced as an important application of knowledge-based AI. It explains how expert systems represent and use **domain knowledge** to solve complex problems that typically require human expertise. The role of **knowledge bases**, inference mechanisms, and **expert system shells** is discussed, highlighting how shells provide a ready-made framework for building expert systems without designing the inference engine from scratch. The chapter also emphasizes **knowledge acquisition**, describing the challenges involved in extracting expert knowledge and encoding it into a form that machines can use effectively. The **explanation facility** of expert systems is presented as a crucial feature that enhances transparency and user trust by justifying the system's conclusions.

Conclusions

This chapter establishes **probability theory and knowledge-based reasoning** as foundational tools for handling uncertainty in artificial intelligence. By quantifying uncertainty and representing expert knowledge explicitly, intelligent systems can make rational decisions even when information is incomplete, imprecise, or unreliable. Probabilistic reasoning provides a powerful complement to logical reasoning, enabling AI systems to function effectively in real-world conditions.

An understanding of probability notation, joint distributions, independence, and Bayes' Rule equips students with essential skills required for advanced AI topics such as **Bayesian networks, decision theory, expert systems, and machine learning**. The probabilistic Wumpus World example demonstrates how uncertainty-aware reasoning significantly improves an agent's performance in complex environments.

Furthermore, the discussion on **Expert Systems** highlights the importance of structured knowledge representation, efficient inference, and effective knowledge acquisition in building intelligent applications. Expert system shells and explanation facilities make such systems practical, reusable, and user-friendly.

In conclusion, uncertainty is not a weakness but a defining characteristic of real-world intelligence.. By embracing uncertainty through probabilistic methods and expert knowledge representation, AI systems become more adaptive, reliable, explainable, and capable of supporting human decision-making in dynamic and imperfect environments.

Chapter Wise Questions

Chapter 1: Artificial Intelligence (AI): Foundations and History

Questions for Review:

1. Define Artificial Intelligence (AI). How does it aim to mimic human thinking and behaviour?
2. What are the foundational disciplines that contribute to the development of AI, and how does each play a role?
3. Explain the significance of natural language processing (NLP) in the evolution of AI. Provide examples of its application in daily life.
4. Discuss the importance of machine learning in the growth of AI. How does it differ from traditional programming?
5. What role does computer vision play in AI, and what are some examples of its impact on industries?
6. How has AI evolved from its early fundamental principles to its present-day applications by 2024?
7. Describe the role of robotics in AI. How does it integrate with other fields like computer science and engineering?
8. Explain how AI is transforming industries and influencing everyday life. Provide at least two examples.
9. What are the historical milestones in the development of AI, and how have they shaped its current state?
10. In your own words, summarize the interdisciplinary nature of AI and its potential to drive future innovations.

Chapter 2: Agents and Environments

Questions for Review:

1. Define an intelligent agent and describe the relationship between an agent and its environment. How do they interact?
2. What is the concept of rationality in the context of intelligent agents? How is it used to evaluate an agent's performance?
3. Explain the different types of environments in which intelligent agents operate. How do properties like observability, determinism, and continuity influence the design of agents?
4. Discuss the structure of agents. What are the key components that make up an intelligent agent?
5. How do simple reflex agents differ from model-based agents? Provide examples to illustrate the differences.
6. What are chatbots, and how do they function as intelligent agents? Give examples of their practical applications.
7. Describe expert systems (ES). What are their main components, and how do they assist in decision-making?
8. What is the role of domain knowledge in expert systems? How is it represented and used effectively?
9. Explain the concept of expert system shells. How do they simplify the development of expert systems?
10. Discuss the process of knowledge acquisition in expert systems. Why is it considered a critical challenge in developing ES?

Chapter 3: Uncertain Knowledge and Reasoning

Questions for Review:

1. Why is quantifying uncertainty important in AI, and how does it enable agents to reason and act effectively in uncertain environments?
2. Define the term "uncertainty" in the context of AI. Provide examples of situations where uncertainty plays a key role.
3. Explain the concept of acting under uncertainty. What challenges do AI agents face in such scenarios?
4. What is basic probability notation, and how is it used to represent uncertain events in AI systems?
5. Discuss the importance of inference using full joint distributions. How do they help in reasoning about multiple variables in uncertain systems?
6. What is the principle of independence in probability theory? How does it simplify the representation and computation of probabilities?
7. State Bayes' Rule. How does it help in updating beliefs based on new evidence?
8. Provide an example of how Bayes' Rule is applied in real-world AI applications, such as spam filtering or medical diagnosis.
9. What are the differences between probability theory and decision theory? How are they integrated in AI for decision-making under uncertainty?
10. Describe how independence assumptions are leveraged by AI developers to simplify the design of systems that handle uncertainty. Why are these assumptions critical for scalability?

Chapter 4: Search Strategies and Logical Agents

Questions for Review:

1. What is the role of search strategies in problem-solving agents, and why are they essential for navigating problem spaces?
2. Differentiate between uninformed and informed search strategies. Provide examples of each type and discuss their applications.
3. Explain the concept of a problem-solving agent. How does it approach finding solutions in a given problem space?
4. What are the key differences between Breadth-First Search (BFS) and Depth-First Search (DFS)? Discuss their advantages and limitations.
5. Describe the Iterative Deepening Depth-First Search (IDDFS) strategy. Why is it considered a hybrid approach, and what are its advantages?
6. What is a heuristic function in the context of informed search strategies? How does it guide the search process?
7. Explain the Greedy Best-First Search strategy. What are its strengths and weaknesses, and how does it rely on heuristics?
8. Discuss the A Search algorithm. How does it combine the concepts of cost and heuristics to find optimal solutions? *
9. Provide examples of real-world problems that can be solved using search strategies. How do these strategies contribute to finding efficient solutions?
10. What are logical agents, and how do they differ from problem-solving agents in their approach to decision-making and reasoning?

Chapter 5: Knowledge-Based Agents and Logical Reasoning

Questions for Review:

1. What is a knowledge-based agent, and how does it use stored knowledge to make decisions and solve problems?
2. Describe the Wumpus World environment. How does it serve as a classic example for reasoning under uncertainty?
3. What are the key differences between propositional logic and first-order logic (FOL)? Provide examples of each.
4. Explain the syntax and semantics of first-order logic (FOL). How do they contribute to the expressive power of FOL compared to propositional logic?
5. What are reasoning patterns in propositional logic? Discuss their significance in AI problem-solving.
6. Define unification in the context of first-order logic. Why is it critical for logical inference?
7. What is forward chaining, and how does it work in first-order logic? Provide an example of its application.
8. Explain backward chaining as a reasoning technique. How does it differ from forward chaining in its approach?
9. Discuss the resolution method in first-order logic. How does it enable inference, and why is it important in AI systems?
10. Compare and contrast propositional inference and first-order inference. What are the strengths and limitations of each?

Index

J

K

L

M

N

O

P

Q

R

S

T

U

V

W

Glossary

A

Accessible Environment – An environment in which an agent can obtain complete and accurate information through its sensors.

Action – An operation performed by an agent that affects the environment.

Adversarial Environment – An environment where agents have opposing goals, such as in competitive games.

Agent – An entity that perceives its environment through sensors and acts upon it using actuators.

Artificial Intelligence (AI) – The branch of computer science concerned with creating systems that exhibit intelligent behaviour.

A* Search – An informed search algorithm that finds optimal solutions using path cost and heuristic estimates.

Agent – An autonomous entity in AI capable of perceiving its environment, reasoning, learning, and acting. See also: Multi-Agent System.

Artificial Intelligence (AI) – Simulation of human intelligence in machines programmed to think, learn, and adapt. See also: Deep Learning, NLP.

B

Backward Chaining – A goal-driven inference technique that works backward from a query to known facts. **Bayes' Rule** – A probabilistic formula used to update beliefs when new evidence is available.

Benign Environment – An environment that does not deliberately oppose the agent.

Breadth First Search (BFS) – An uninformed search strategy that explores nodes level by level.

C

Collaborative Environment – An environment where multiple agents cooperate to achieve a common goal.

Competitive Environment – An environment where agents compete against each other.

Conditional Probability – The probability of an event given that another event has occurred.

Continuous Environment – An environment with infinitely many states or actions.

Chatbot – AI-powered software designed to simulate conversations with human users via text or voice. See also: NLP.

Cognitive Science – The interdisciplinary study of mind and intelligence, including psychology, neuroscience, and AI.

D

Depth First Search (DFS) – An uninformed search strategy that explores as far as possible along a branch before backtracking.

Deterministic Environment – An environment where actions have predictable outcomes.

Discrete Environment – An environment with a finite number of states, actions, or time steps.

Dynamic Environment – An environment that can change while the agent is making decisions.

Deep Learning – A subset of machine learning using neural networks for complex pattern recognition. See also: Neural Network.

Decision Theory – A framework for rational decision-making in uncertain environments.

E

Episodic Environment – An environment where each action is independent of previous actions.

Environment – Everything external to an agent that it interacts with.

Explanation Facility – A component of an expert system that explains how conclusions are derived.

Expert System – A computer system that emulates the decision-making ability of a human expert.

Expert System Shell – A generic expert system framework that provides inference mechanisms without domain knowledge.

Expert System – AI programs that emulate human expertise for decision-making and problem-solving. See also: Utility-Based Agent.

F

First Order Logic (FOL) – A formal language used to represent objects, relationships, and quantifiers.

Forward Chaining – A data-driven inference method that derives conclusions from known facts.

Fully Observable Environment – An environment where the agent can perceive the complete state.

Fully Observable Environment – An environment where an agent has complete access to all relevant information at any given time. See also: Partially Observable Environment.

G

Goal-Based Agent – An agent that selects actions based on achieving specific goals.

Greedy Best-First Search – An informed search strategy that expands the node closest to the goal using a heuristic.

Goal-Based Agent – An agent that evaluates actions based on their ability to achieve specific objectives. See also: Utility-Based Agent.

H

Heuristic Function – A function that estimates the cost to reach the goal from a given state.

History of AI – The development of artificial intelligence from early symbolic systems to modern approaches.

I

Inaccessible Environment – An environment where complete information is not available to the agent.

Independence – A condition where one variable does not affect another.

Inference – The process of deriving new information from known knowledge.

Inference Engine – The reasoning component of an expert system.

Informed Search Strategy – A search strategy that uses heuristics to guide exploration.

Intelligent Agent – An agent that acts rationally to maximize performance.

J

Joint Probability Distribution – A probability distribution over multiple random variables.

K

Knowledge Acquisition – The process of capturing expert knowledge for use in an expert system.

Knowledge Acquisition Bottleneck – The difficulty of extracting and formalizing expert knowledge.

Knowledge Base – A repository of facts and rules used by an AI system.

Knowledge-Based Agent – An agent that reasons using stored knowledge.

Known Environment – An environment where the rules and outcomes are known to the agent.

L

Learning Agent – An agent that improves its performance through experience.

Logic – A formal system for reasoning and inference.

Logical Agent – An agent that uses logic to reason about actions and outcomes.

Learning Agent – An AI system that improves performance over time by learning from past experiences.

M

Model-Based Reflex Agent – An agent that maintains an internal model of the environment.

Multi-Agent System – A system in which multiple agents interact in the same environment.

Model-Based Agent – An AI agent that uses an internal model to handle partially observable environments. See also: Reflex Agent.

Multi-Agent System – A collection of autonomous agents interacting to achieve individual or collective goals. See also: Agent.

N

Natural Language Processing (NLP) – The branch of AI focused on interaction between computers and human language. See also: Chatbot

Neural Network – A computational model inspired by the human brain, used extensively in deep learning. See also: Deep Learning.

O

Observation – Information perceived by an agent from the environment.

P

Partially Observable Environment – An environment where the agent has incomplete information.

Performance Measure – A criterion used to evaluate an agent's success.

Problem-Solving Agent – An agent that uses search techniques to find solutions.

Propositional Logic – A logic system based on propositions that are either true or false.

Partially Observable Environment – An environment where an agent has limited information about the current state. See also: Fully Observable Environment.

Q

Quantifying Uncertainty – Representing uncertainty using probabilities.

R

Rational Agent – An agent that chooses actions to maximize expected performance.

Reasoning – The process of drawing conclusions from knowledge.

Reflex Agent (Simple Reflex Agent) – An agent that selects actions based only on the current percept.

Resolution – A rule of inference used in propositional and first-order logic.

Reinforcement Learning – Machine learning where agents learn optimal behavior through rewards and penalties. See also: Supervised Learning, Unsupervised Learning.

Reflex Agent – An agent that selects actions based on predefined rules, without memory or learning. See also: Model-Based Agent.

S

Search Space – The set of all possible states reachable from an initial state.

Sequential Environment – An environment where current actions affect future states.

Single-Agent Environment – An environment containing only one agent.

Static Environment – An environment that does not change during decision-making.

Stochastic Environment – An environment with uncertain outcomes.

Stochastic Environment – An environment that involves randomness and uncertainty in state transitions.

Supervised Learning – A machine learning approach using labeled data to train models for specific tasks. See also: Unsupervised Learning, Reinforcement Learning.

T

Total Turing Test – An extended version of the Turing Test that evaluates not only a machine's conversational ability but also its perception, learning, and physical interaction with the real world, requiring capabilities such as vision, speech recognition, and motor control.

Truth Value – Indicates whether a proposition is true or false.

Turing Test – A test proposed by Alan Turing to evaluate a machine's intelligence based on its ability to exhibit human-like behaviour in a text-based conversation with a human evaluator, such that the evaluator cannot reliably distinguish the machine from a human.

U

Unification – The process of making logical expressions identical.

Uninformed Search Strategy – A search strategy that does not use heuristics.

Unknown Environment – An environment where the agent does not know the rules in advance.

Utility-Based Agent – An agent that selects actions to maximize a utility function.

Unsupervised Learning – A machine learning technique for discovering patterns in data without labeled outputs. See also: Supervised Learning, Reinforcement Learning.

Utility-Based Agent – An agent that evaluates outcomes using a utility function to select actions maximizing utility. See also: Expert System, Goal-Based Agent.

W

Wumpus World – A classic AI problem used to illustrate logical reasoning.

Wumpus World Revisited – A probabilistic version of the Wumpus World for reasoning under uncertainty.